LIL' REV TEACHES

CLAWHAMMER UKULELE

A BEGINNER'S GUIDE

To access video, visit:
www.halleonard.com/mylibrary

Enter Code
4835-8062-2168-8246

Front Cover Photo by Mariela Revenson

Video Performance by Lil' Rev
Guitar Accompaniment by Will Branch
Video by DV Productions - Milwaukee, WI

ISBN 978-1-70513-454-2

Visit Hal Leonard Online at **www.halleonard.com**

World headquarters, contact:
Hal Leonard
7777 West Bluemound Road
Milwaukee, WI 53213
Email: info@halleonard.com

In Europe, contact:
Hal Leonard Europe Limited
Dettingen Way
Bury St Edmunds, Suffolk, IP33 3YB
Email: info@halleonardeurope.com

In Australia, contact:
Hal Leonard Australia Pty. Ltd.
4 Lentara Court
Cheltenham, Victoria, 3192 Australia
Email: info@halleonard.com.au

CONTENTS

INTRODUCTION 

Photo by Chyrisse Tabone. Used with permission.

Howdy Ukulele Friends,

Allow me to make a bold statement: Learning the clawhammer stroke is going to change your life!

It'll open up a whole new musical world that can't be had using single-string melody playing techniques, chord-melody style, or even fingerstyle approaches. If you are interested in playing old-time string-band music, bluegrass, folk, country western, and yes, even blues, the clawhammer stroke will provide a brand-new way to play your arrangements.

The clawhammer stroke has a propulsive, toe-tapping brilliance that's inherent in its sound and delivery. It is unmistakable, authentic, and genuinely rooted in tradition, yet totally open to wherever you'd like to take it in the future. Furthermore, the re-entrant high-G string of the soprano- and concert-sized ukuleles allows for a banjo-like drone that's necessary to create this timeless sound.

While the initial learning curve requires some patience, persistence pays big dividends when you finally have your "now I get it" moment and the sound that you've been painstakingly striving towards—via the "bum-ditty" stroke, melodic clawhammer exercises, and the method outlined in these pages—comes to fruition.

I'll never forget the sunny summer day that I learned to play clawhammer on the banjo, o'er in the bluff country of Spring Grove, Minnesota, from old-time fiddler and banjo player Gail Heil. I must have been a tough student because I could see the consternation in Gail's eyes as I tried to replicate what she was trying to show me. Still, I was determined to learn to play clawhammer, and Gail was a great teacher. I am one of thousands of students that she shared her gift of old-time music with, and therein lies the beauty of this style. Once you get some tunes under your belt, there is a whole world of people to play music with who love to jam the old fiddle tunes and sing high harmony while you claw out "Rolling in My Sweet Baby's Arms," or just sit on the front porch and make some homemade music together.

If you have questions along the way, visit me at: **www.lilrev.com**. In the meantime, keep your skillet good and greasy!

—Lil' Rev

ABOUT THE VIDEO LESSONS

The video lessons that come with this book are integral to your success in learning the clawhammer technique! All the videos are available for streaming or download on the Hal Leonard My Library website. Simply visit **www.halleonard.com/mylibrary** and enter the unique 16-digit code, located on page 1 of this book, to gain access.

In the book, examples and topics with accompanying video lessons will have this video symbol:

AN ABBREVIATED BANJO HISTORY

The re-entrant high-G string on the ukulele allows it to act as a drone in the same manner that the 5-string banjo utilizes the 5th peg to help achieve its distinctive sound. In order for us to understand how this stroke came to be, it's important to understand a little bit about the banjo and its humble beginnings in America.

It's no secret that the earliest incarnation of the banjo originated in West Africa. Early-American instruments made from gourds with long, stick-shaped necks, raccoon-, cat-, or calf-skin heads, and horse-hair strings began to appear in print and artwork as early as the mid-1700s in early America.

Today, if you go searching for a direct link between the banjo and its West African roots, you will more than likely wind up in Senegal, where the Senegambian instrument, known as the *akonting* (*ekonting*), not only looks but sounds a lot like a distant relative of the banjo with its gourd-shaped body, pole-shaped neck, carved bridge, and gut strings. Often referred to as a *bandore*, *banza*, or *banjar* by early players, the banjo has traveled a long and innovative road, while always remaining true to its roots.

By the mid-1800s, the banjo had become a mainstay of American culture, bringing with it an explosion in factory-made banjos, though most were made in relatively small shops. The instruments of this era displayed a vast improvement in quality, i.e., rims, tooling, pegs, tone-rings, and more! Philadelphia banjo manufacturer S.S. Stewart was the most prominent builder of this time period, as well as Fairbanks and Cole, located in Boston, Massachusetts.

Just prior to the Civil War, as the banjo craze was widening its reach, Oliver Ditson, Tom Briggs, Phil Rice, and James Buckley all published some of the earliest banjo instruction books, starting in 1855 with Oliver Ditson and soon thereafter with books by Dan Emmett and many others.

It's hard to imagine banjo glee clubs proliferating at colleges across America, like the Yale Banjo Club, circa 1894. Ushered in alongside the sentimental song era of the 1890s, songs of the old home place, mom and dad, and unrequited love were all tucked neatly into the piano bench. Soon, America's fascination with the banjo began to show up in pop culture. Banjo orchestras also came of age in this era, giving credence to a whole cottage industry of teachers, builders, entertainers, and players.

Banjo styles evolved from the highly syncopated, up-and-down stroke playing of the early years to include classical-, ragtime-, and blues-inspired players. Appalachian traditions gave way to both two- and three-finger styles, and much later, the bluegrass influence of Earl Scruggs' innovative banjo-roll style. Clawhammer ukulele, as a tradition, has only recently begun to flower in the last decade or so in the hands of players like Cathy Fink, the Canote Brothers, Aaron Keim, Ken Middleton, and yours truly!

Welcome to the golden era of clawhammer ukulele!

CHOOSING THE RIGHT UKULELE FOR CLAWHAMMER

The number-one question asked amongst beginning clawhammer players is: **What type of ukulele is best for playing clawhammer?**

Before you can begin playing clawhammer on the ukulele, there are a few important things to consider, the first of which is your G string!

If you look closely at a 5-string banjo, you'll see that the 5th string is shorter than the rest. It's attached on the left side of the neck, midway down, and separate from those on the headstock. This string, which is known as the *drone string*, is responsible for the distinctive sound of the banjo.

Photo courtesy of the Rik Palieri Archive. Used with permission.

In order to produce this type of droning sound on the little nylon-string ukulele, you've got to use a traditional, re-entrant, high G for your 4th string (the string on top, or closest to your face, when holding the instrument). By using the high-G string, the drone will ring out in a high enough octave to ride above the other three. When the technique is done right, it produces a galloping sound that carries the melody and rhythm right along.

The second thing that is important to consider is the scale length of your ukulele.

There are plenty of cool tenor ukes and banjo ukes on the market that sound great, but it's the author's opinion that, when it comes to the ukulele, the shorter scale of the concert- and soprano-sized ukes produce more than enough tension to create a really tight clawhammer sound.

The longer scale, especially on a nylon-strung, wood-bodied tenor, just doesn't offer enough tension to produce a brilliant clawhammer sound. Tenor banjo ukuleles sound a little brighter, but ultimately, you're going to get the best sound out of a soprano- or concert-scale uke.

CLAWHAMMER PLAYING POSITION AND TUNINGS

The best playing position for learning clawhammer ukulele is seated with a strap on the instrument. The ukulele, like the banjo, rests gently on your upper thigh when seated, or, if you should choose to stand, then the strap will support your instrument as it hangs snug against your stomach/chest.

UKULELE TUNINGS FOR CLAWHAMMER

There are many tunings that work well with the clawhammer technique on the ukulele. The most common is the standard re-entrant ukulele tuning of G-C-E-A (listed 4th string to 1st string) or "C tuning." Below is a list of tunings and how to use them.

1. **GCEA Tuning** (Standard Tuning, C6 Tuning, "C Tuning"): If you choose to keep the ukulele in standard tuning, you'll do well to play in the keys of G and C, which will allow you to use the G for droning. One of the most common tunings on the banjo is G tuning, which the ukulele does well in C tuning by utilizing the open G chord. Most of what we'll do in this book will utilize standard GCEA tuning. Once your skills improve, you can move on to the keys of F, A, and C in C tuning.
2. **GCEG Tuning** (Open C Tuning): By tuning the 1st string down one whole step, from A to G, we create an open C chord (the notes in a C chord are C-E-G). This is great for *frailing* songs in C or G, a down-strummed form of rhythmic old-time and bluegrass accompaniment.
3. **GBDG Tuning** (Open G Tuning): This tuning allows you to play really nice moveable *barre chords* (chords that are fretted by laying one finger across more than one string at a time) as well as utilize more open-string possibilities when arranging tunes in open G.
4. **ADF♯B Tuning** (D6 Tuning, "D Tuning"): This is used as the main tuning in Canada and other parts of the world. It allows for a brighter, punchier sound, being one whole step up from C6 tuning. It also has the added bonus of being in the banjo- and fiddle-friendly key of D. You'll want to play with this tuning a bit, if for no other reason than it's a very common key. Fiddle tunes in D work much better in this tuning than in GCEA. The usual C chord shapes and positions become D chords in this tuning, and likewise, G shapes become A chords and F shapes become G chords.

Like the banjo, the ukulele can be tuned in a multitude of different ways, each offering a new world of possibilities. These four offer a great place to start!

LEARNING THE BUM-DITTY STROKE

"Bum-ditty" is an important stroke that you'll need to learn in order to play clawhammer. It consists of three parts that combine to form one stroke. "Bum-dit-ty" is also the sound that the stroke makes when done properly.

BASIC HAND POSITION

To start the clawhammer stroke, you'll need to choose between two different options for your hand shape and position. I suggest you experiment with each, and then pick either shape #1 or shape #2, sticking to your choice until you achieve a good level of proficiency.

Claw shape #1 uses the nail side of the index finger to strike single notes and chords; claw shape #2 uses the nail side of the middle finger to strike single notes and chords. Look at the pictures below to see how this looks, then watch the video for this lesson to dig a little deeper.

Claw Shape #1 - Index Finger

Claw Shape #2 - Middle Finger

Whether you choose #1 or #2, I want to make it clear that you're using both the tip of the fingernail as well as the fleshy part of the fingertip to strike a note or chord.

- In shape #1, the remaining fingers can either be left curled up or you can let them hang down.
- In shape #2, the index hangs down while the middle finger does all the work, and the ring and pinky remain curled up.

Both shapes, when applied, share the same downward hammering motion that pivots from a combination of the elbow and wrist. The thumb is cocked slightly, over the G string, with the fleshy pad of the thumb dropping down on the string and gently lifting off.

Basic Stroke Exercise

Watch the video to practice your first exercise: a muted clawhammer stroke. For now, mute the strings with your fretting hand so they don't ring; we're just focusing on the clawhammer hand with this exercise. Follow the steps below and on screen.

1. Strike down on the 3rd string (C string) with your finger.
2. Brush down on the 3rd, 2nd, and 1st strings (C-E-A strings) in one full movement with the same finger, allowing your thumb to drop down on the 4th string (G string).
3. Lift your thumb off of the 4th string to create a "pop"; as it lifts off each time, it creates a galloping sound.

BUM-DITTY EXERCISES

There are three unique movements that make up clawhammer's signature stroke. Here they are as applied to a G chord:

1. The index or middle finger strikes the D note of the G chord (2nd fret, C string).
2. The index or middle finger brushes down across the G chord (strings 3, 2, and 1).
3. The thumb comes to rest on the G string (string 4), pressing down and out slightly, and then lifting off.

When combined together, the sound the stroke makes is "bum-dit-ty, bum-dit-ty, bum-dit-ty, bum-dit-ty." Here's the exercise as described above. When starting out, this is the single most important exercise.

G Chord Exercise

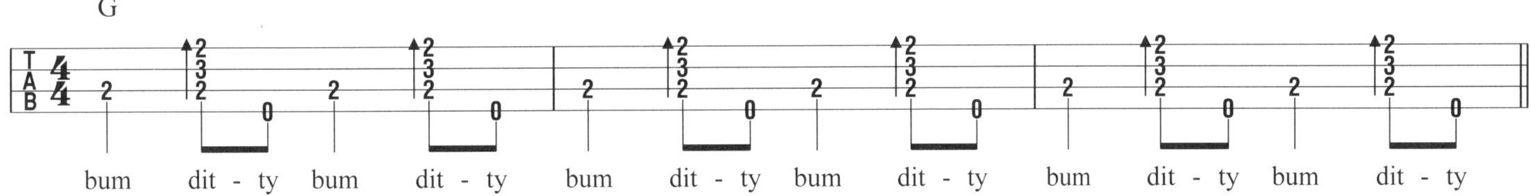

Now let's add another chord to our basic bum-ditty.

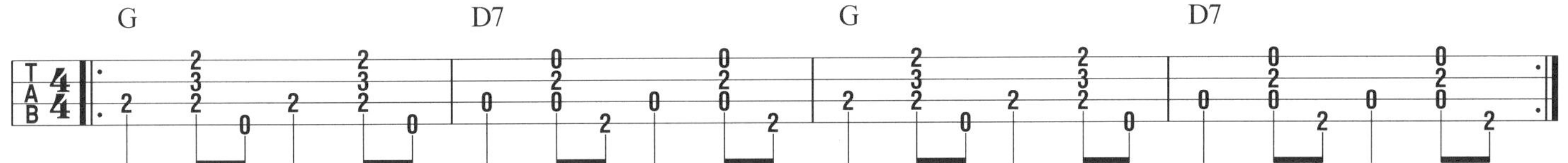

Gradually, add more chords to your practice. Then you'll be ready for all kinds of songs, including those with many chord changes or those with just a few! Now let's try G, C, and D7:

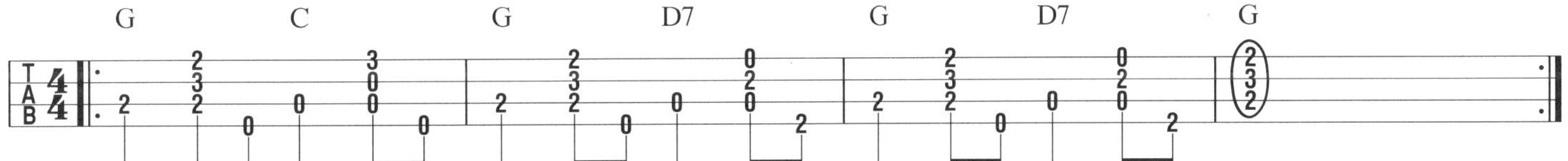

Next, practice this stroke on just the C chord, and then try going back and forth between the C and G7 chords.

C Chord Exercise

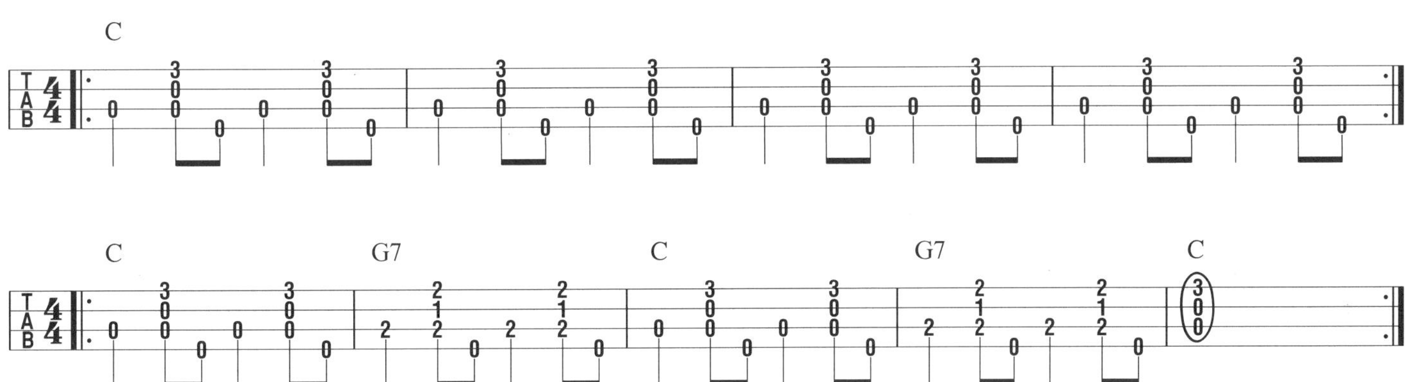

REFINING YOUR BUM-DITTY STROKE: SINGLE-NOTE STUDIES

As mentioned earlier, learning the bum-ditty stroke requires mastery of three different skill sets:

1. **Playing single notes** using the index or middle finger on the down stroke. This is the "bum" in the bum-ditty. For example, if playing a G chord, you'd start by striking the 2nd fret of the C string, which is a D note.
2. **Brushing chords** effectively with the index or middle finger.
3. **Droning on the G string** using the thumb and perfecting the drone's unique on/off pattern.

In the following exercises, we'll start with a few examples designed to help you master single notes (with no brush and no drone). After some single-note practice, we'll isolate the brush stroke, then combine single notes with drones, and finally, all three skills combined.

Play the basic G major scale along one string, using your index or middle finger with no drone and all down strokes:

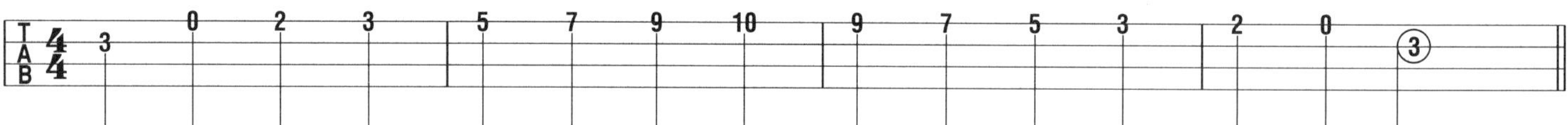

Great job playing the G major scale. Now, let's try to play a super-easy fiddle tune called "Boil 'Em Cabbage Down" using your index or middle finger to play single notes.

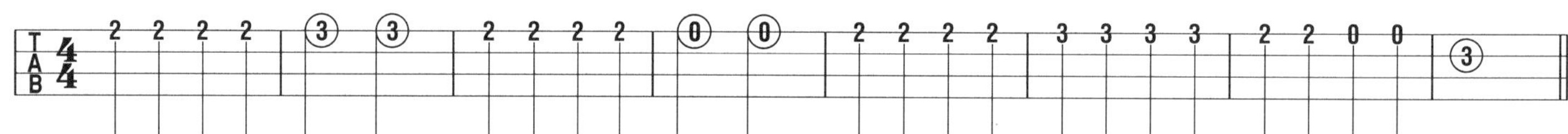

Continuing our single-note studies without using drone or brush strokes, this time we'll focus on moving the G scale up the neck on the E string.

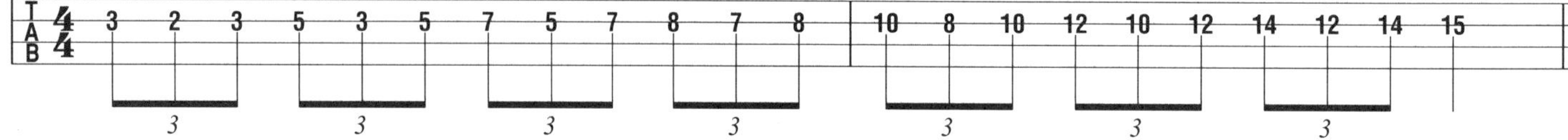

REFINING YOUR BUM-DITTY STROKE: THE BRUSH STROKE

The brush stroke is the second of three movements in bum-ditty.

Banjo players refer to the bum-ditty stroke as "note-strum-drone." Each of these three actions is essential to the overall sound and rhythm of the stroke, and each requires repetition to master. The following exercises and accompanying video will help you dial in a good, solid brush stroke. Be sure to play through these exercises as much as possible, as they'll form the foundation of your bum-ditty.

The first brush stroke exercise is a two-chord strum using G and D7. You'll find brush strokes are often integrated into fiddle-tune arrangements and they also make good accompaniment skill-builders as well. Count "1-2-3-4" for each measure and use either your index or middle finger to brush each chord.

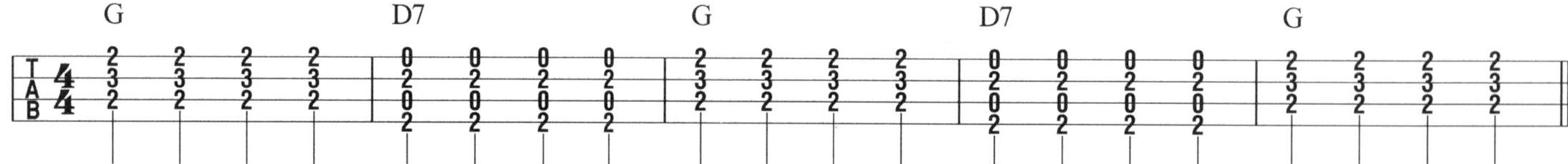

This exercise utilizes the G, C, and D7 chords. Strike each chord and count "**1**-2-**3**-4." The emphasis on beats 1 and 3 helps to reinforce that each chord will be played two times per measure.

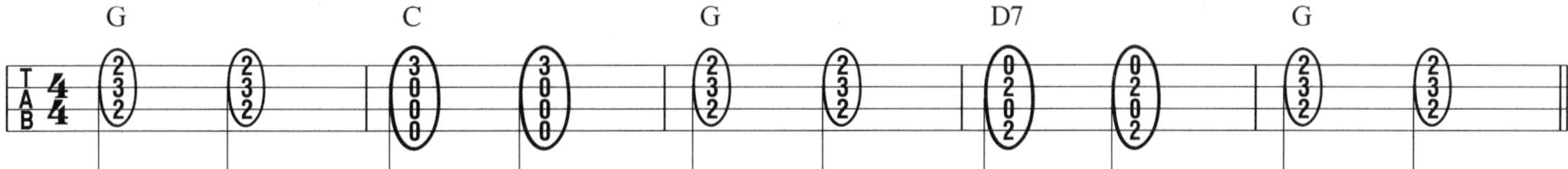

Next is an exercise that draws its chordal influence from the ragtime era of the early 1900s. It also illustrates the challenges of learning to develop a solid brush stroke, even when the chords are changing multiple times within each measure.

The Ragtime Way

Here's a different way to practice your brush stroke. Sing "The Crawdad Song" and change chords as they appear above the lyrics. As before, play straight down strokes with the index or middle finger.

The Crawdad Song

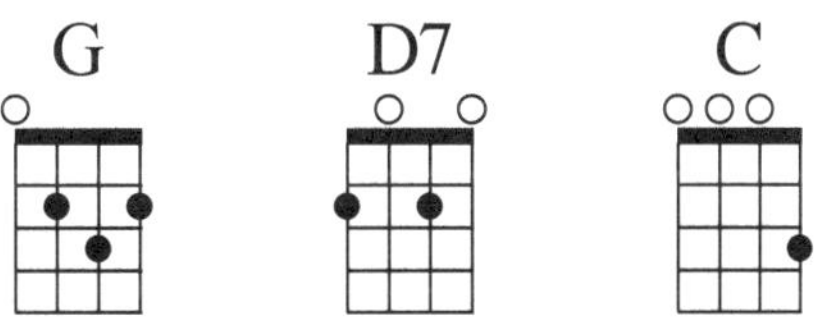

G
You get a line and I'll get a pole now, honey.

D7
Honey, you get a line and I'll get a pole now, babe, babe.

G **C**
You get a line and I'll get a pole, we'll go fishing in the crawdad hole,

G **D7** **G**
Honey, sugar baby, mine.

Extra Verses:
Yonder come a man with a sack on his back now, honey. (2x)
Yonder come a man with a sack on his back, packing all the crawdads he can pack.
Honey, sugar baby, mine.

What you gonna do when the lake runs dry now, honey? (2x)
What you gonna do when the lake runs dry now, sit on the banks and watch the crawdads dry?
Honey, sugar baby, mine.

REFINING YOUR BUM-DITTY STROKE: ADDING THE DRONE

Now it's time to learn how to play a strong, steady drone on your high-G string. Remember, the drone is the last of the three movements in the stroke. Just as you begin to finish brushing the G chord, your thumb is dropping down onto the G string. A small amount of pressure is applied, and as you lift off, you'll push the string outwards a tiny bit. This push outward is very subtle and usually just looks like you are simply lifting off the string; you really can't see the pushing outwards of the G string, but it's there! This is the one technique in the stroke that requires a lot of practice to master... but alas! If you stay with it and don't give up, soon you'll start to feel the driving rhythm that's inherent when one can keep a steady drone going.

This first exercise removes the "note-strum" parts of the stroke, prior to the drone. Here we'll isolate the drone, thereby giving you a chance to focus exclusively on the mechanics of it. Count "1, 2, 3, 4" as you play through it.

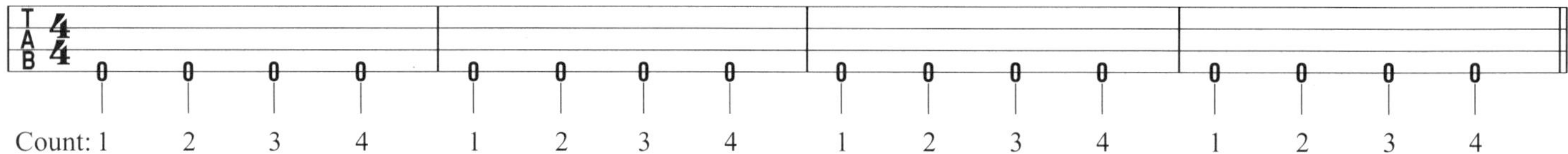

Please spend a lot of time practicing the previous exercise, with its four drone beats per measure, before you attempt to double them up in the next exercise. Here we go from playing quarter notes to eighth notes, turning four drones per measure into eight. Watch the video a few times and then give it your best shot! Count "1 and, 2 and, 3 and, 4 and" for each bar.

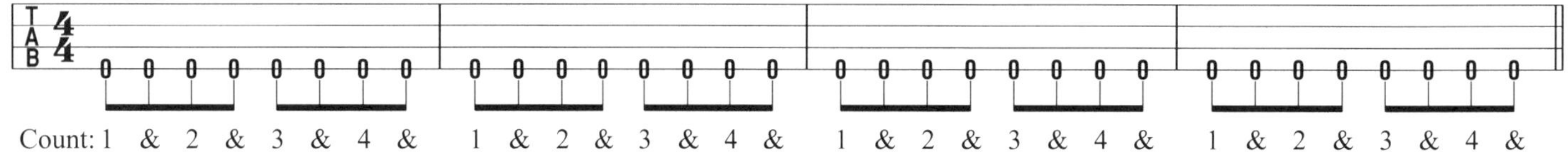

This exercise is an extended study in combining the drone and the individual notes which mimic the bum-ditty sound, minus the brush stroke. This will also teach you how to move across all three melody strings. Say "bum-dit-ty" as you go along.

Combining Notes and Drones

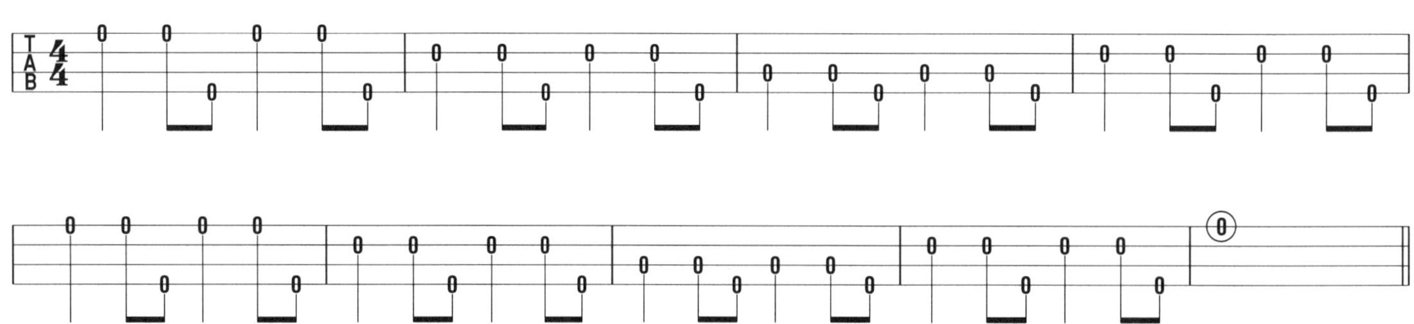

Let's practice the G major scale with a drone following each scale tone. Count "1 and, 2 and, 3 and, 4 and" for each bar.

Droning the G Scale

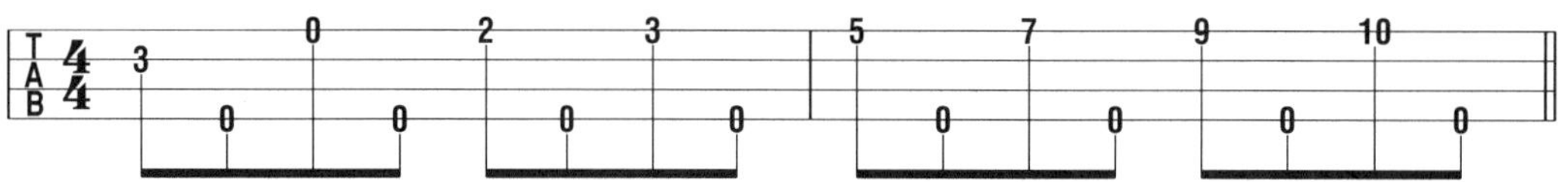

Alright, now let's revisit the melody of the old classic "Boil 'Em Cabbage Down," now with added drones. Count "1 and, 2 and, 3 and, 4 and."

Boil 'Em Cabbage Drone

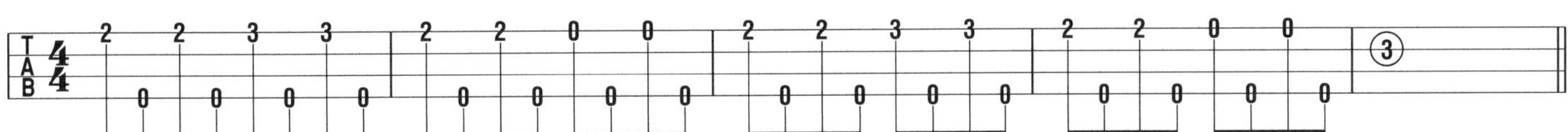

MORE DRONE EXERCISES AND SONGS

The drone is the heart and soul of the clawhammer sound. It's also the most challenging aspect of the bum-ditty stroke (or "note-strum-drone"). Let's spend a little more time learning to add a strong drone component to your clawhammer playing.

You can't play this next exercise too many times. It's super basic, but all roads lead to clawhammer bliss when you practice this one repetitively.

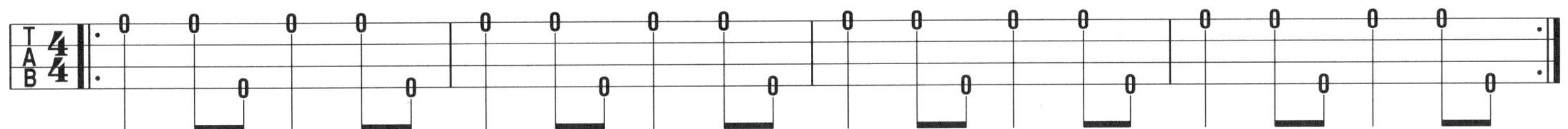

Here's an old, familiar children's play song that makes for great beginning drone practice.

Frère Jacques

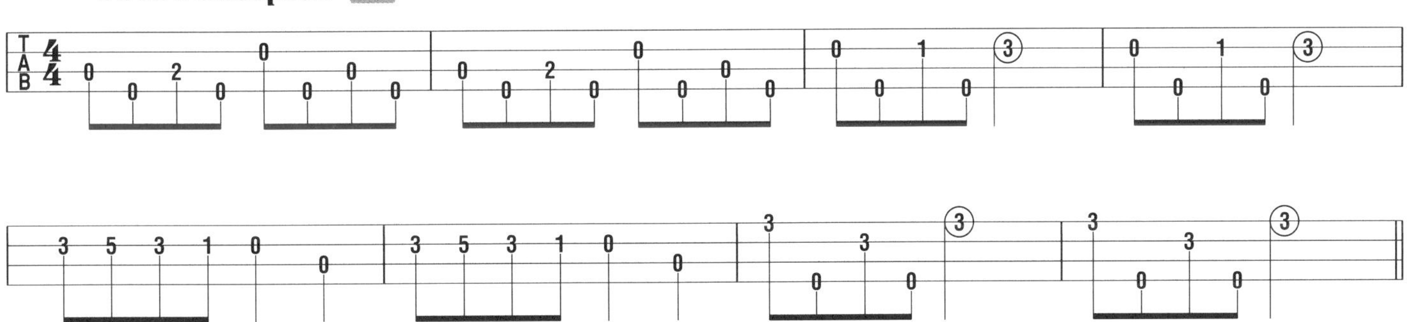

A *double stop* means you play two notes at the same time. This next exercise follows the G major scale with single notes, double stops, and drones.

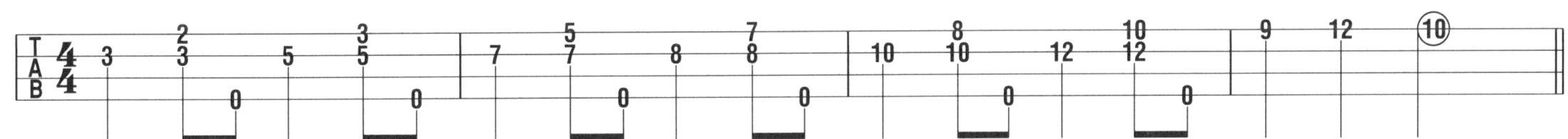

It's a lot of fun to build your skills with old, familiar melodies like "Mary Had a Little Lamb," and easy to tell if you've made a mistake!

Mary Had a Little Lamb

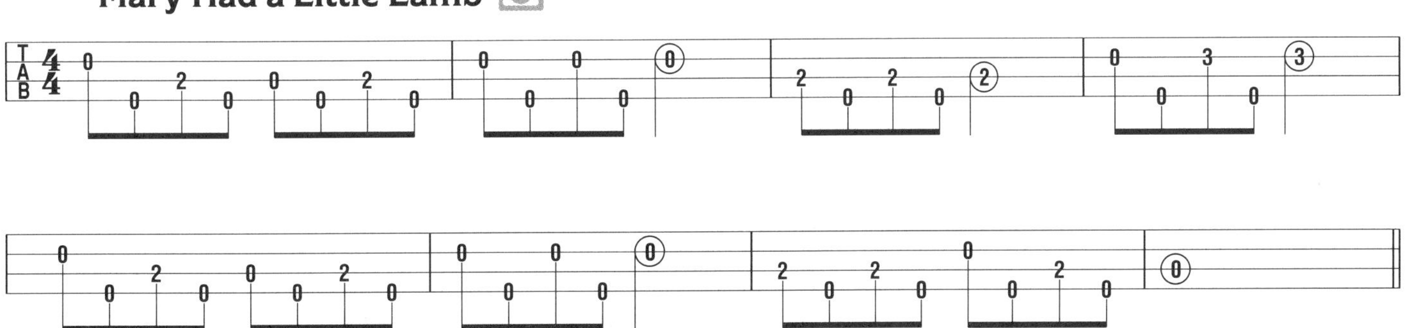

VARYING THE DRONE WITH SIMPLE MELODIES

As you get more comfortable using your thumb to drone on the high-G string, you'll soon discover that some melodies don't necessarily need a lot of drone. On the contrary, as you become extremely proficient as a clawhammer player, you'll be capable of adding almost constant drone, if that's what a tune calls for.

Below is a warm-up exercise that uses the classic Beethoven melody "Ode to Joy." Notice that there are no drone notes. The purpose of this exercise is to help you develop finger agility and accuracy when striking a melody note with the fingernail. Remember, clawhammer means that there's a hammering motion; this motion should pivot from the wrist. Watch the video and focus on how the wrist and elbow effect the instrument, and also how the fingernail strikes the string.

Ode to Joy

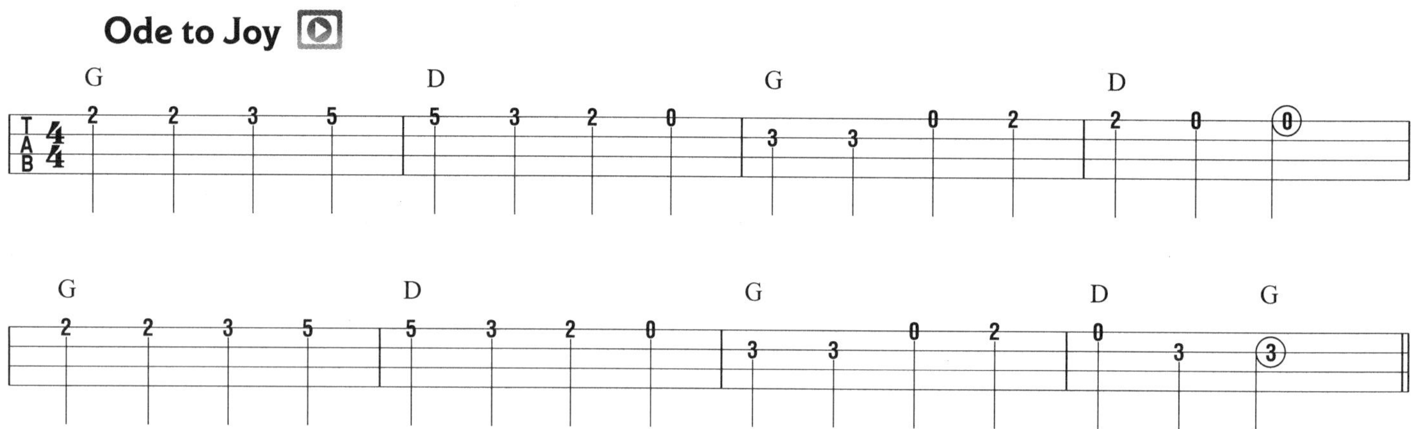

"Go Tell Aunt Rhody" is a beloved children's melody, popular in Appalachian circles and often picked by banjo players when singing for kids at play. Just one drone is added to the end here for a nice effect.

Go Tell Aunt Rhody

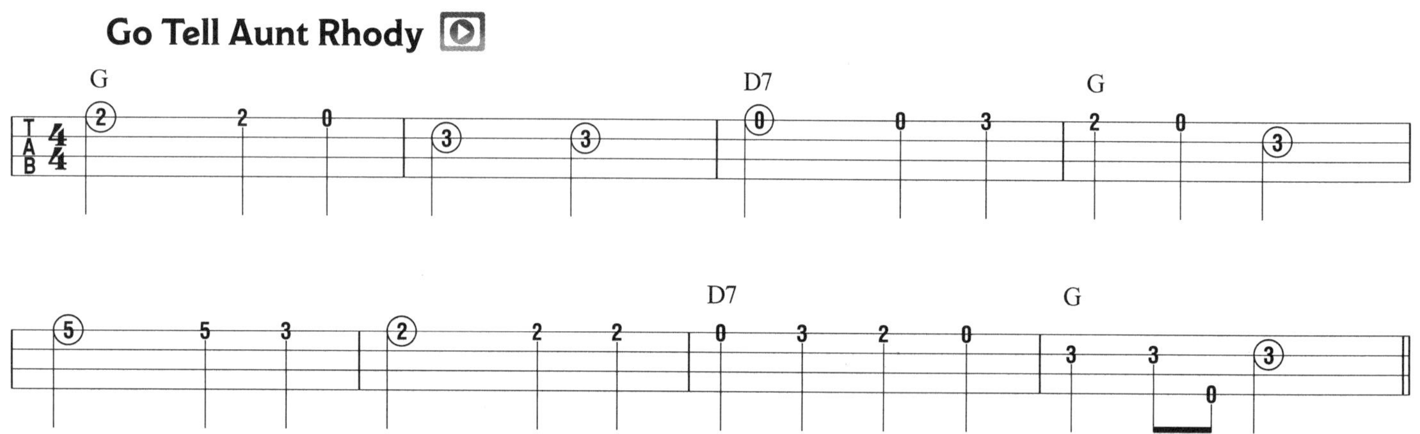

Here's another old-time favorite dating back to the late 1800s. It's still around today because it's a catchy little melody. It doesn't require a lot of drone notes and can be used to perfect your melody, drone, and brush stroke playing.

Goodnight, Ladies

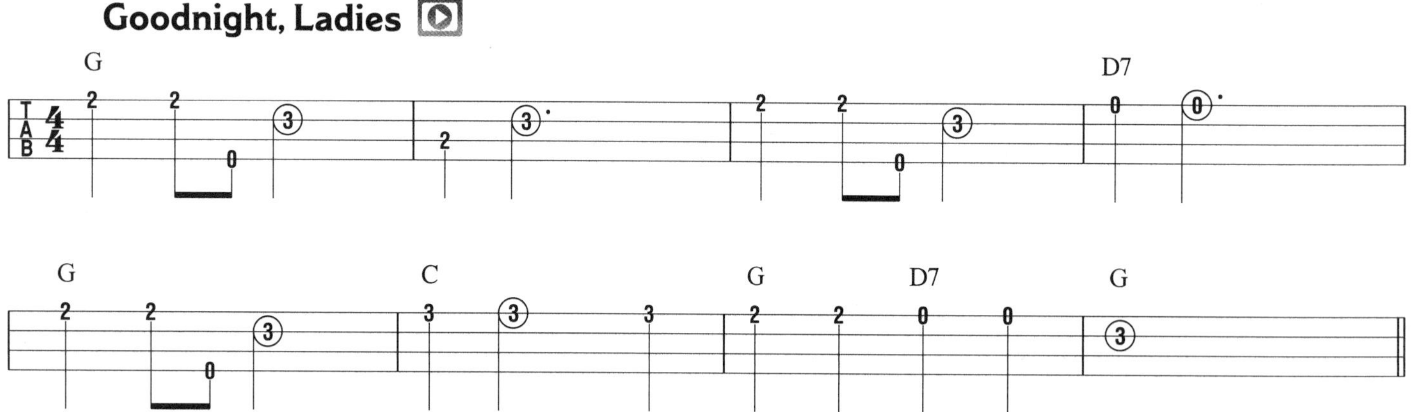

PLAYING FIDDLE TUNES IN G WITH BASIC DRONES

OLD JOE CLARK

"Old Joe Clark" is one of the most studied fiddle tunes, especially amongst those just getting started on building a repertoire of this material. It has a catchy, memorable melody that isn't too complicated and can be played with a minimal number of drones, making this an easy feather in the beginning clawhammer player's cap. This tune is so common that it's unlikely to be missing from the pages of any clawhammer, bluegrass, or old-time string-band tune book, and most certainly will appear at your next jam, festival, or parking-lot-picker's circle. One might even say that learning this tune is a must!

To begin, please review this previous drone exercise (shown again below). Play it over and over until it feels comfortable. This exercise will help you get the feel for the bum-ditty drones that appear in measures 2, 6, 12, and 16 of "Old Joe Clark."

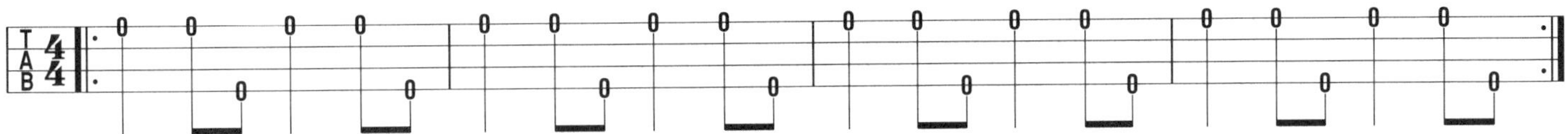

As you begin to work through this piece, focus on playing clean single-note phrases, like the ones that appear in measures 1 and 4, for example. Combine this with a solid understanding of the exercise above and you'll be rocking this tune like a pro in no time!

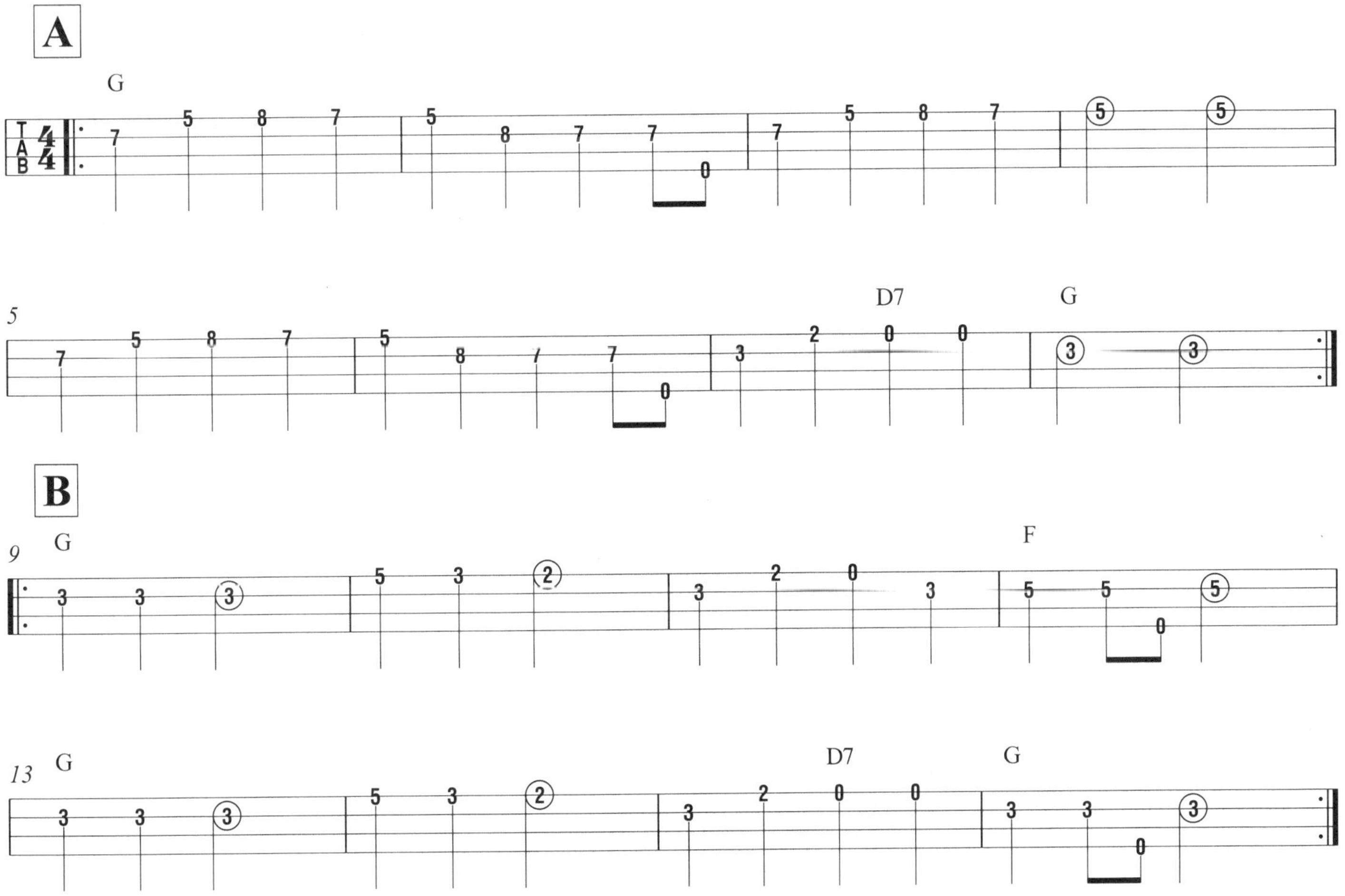

A

G

5 D7 G

B

9 G F

13 G D7 G

DAVY, DAVY

"Davy, Davy" is a traditional instrumental dance tune that dates back to the late 1800s. It is part of a family of related traditional tunes including "Going Down the River," "Sailing Down the River," and "Paddy Won't You Drink Some Cider."

Most of us who fall in love with old-time music find local sources to inspire us, and I'm no exception. I first heard this tune played by one of Milwaukee's finest old-time clawhammer players, John Nicholson of the band Frogwater. Later, I discovered early sources like those recorded by banjoist Bob Carlin, the New Lost City Ramblers, and the Weems String Band.

The melody to this tune is very simple and incredibly catchy. It's shown here first without drones, then with added drones. This is a great way to learn a tune when you are just starting out, as it allows you to soak up a new melody without having to think much about the drone; once you have it down, then you can build upon the basic melody by practicing it with the added drones.

Note: This tune is written in *2/4 time*. A time signature of 2/4 means that there are two quarter notes in each measure.

To begin, first listen and watch the video to absorb the melody. Once the tune is in your ear, focus on striking each note clearly with your nail/fingertip. Remember to use a hammer-like motion to stroke down on each note. Lastly, remember that each section repeats twice.'

Davy, Davy (No Drone Version)

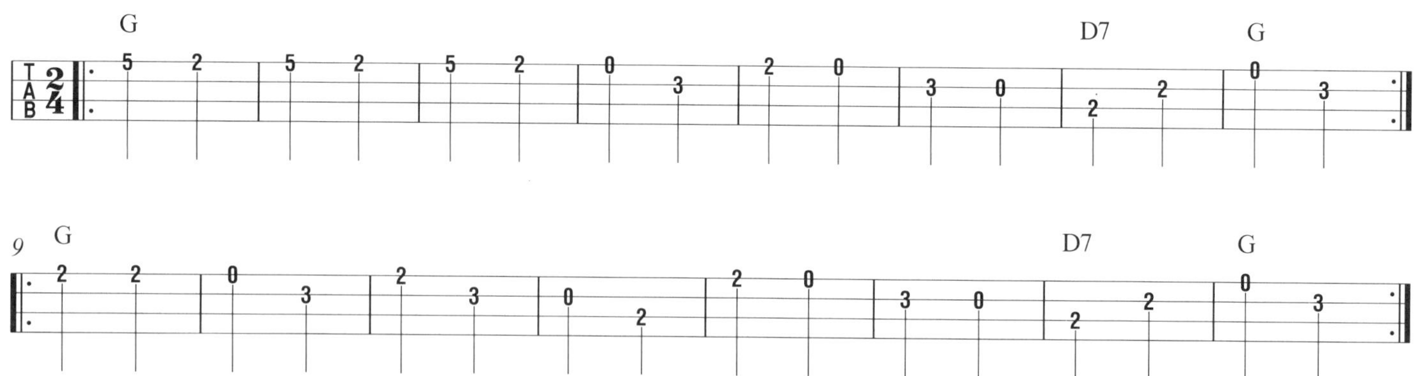

Davy, Davy (Drone Version)

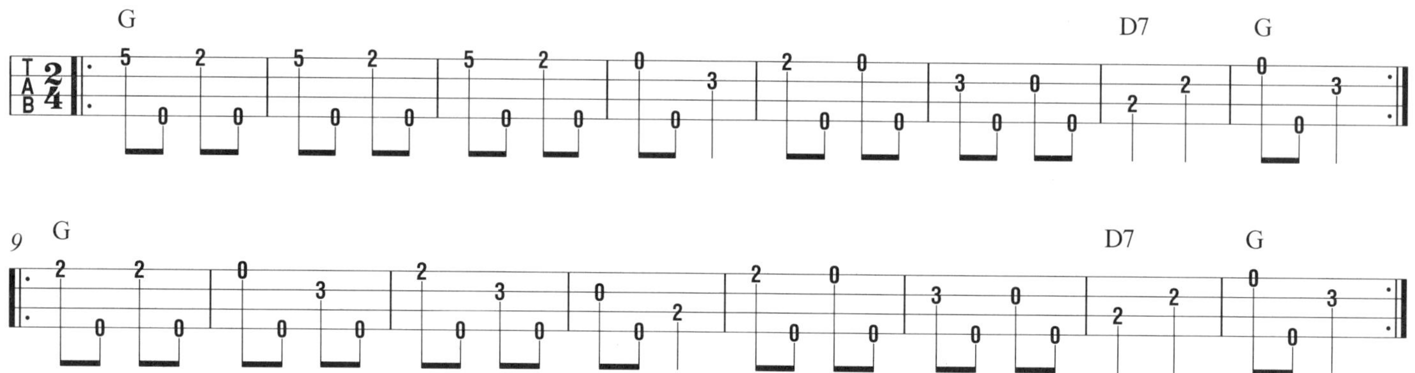

BRUSHING CHORDS WITH MELODY

Clawhammer 101 dictates that we first become proficient at picking single-string melodies with and without a drone. Once we've got the stroke down and have learned the basic brush stroke that's inherent in the bum-ditty, then it's time to learn how to integrate both melody and chord-brushing into one. Ultimately, this will help your arrangements sound much fuller.

TOM DOOLEY

"Tom Dooley" is a simple folk melody dating back to the late 1800s. This arrangement combines single-string melody playing with sparse droning and some basic brushing on the G chord. Start slowly, playing and repeating each measure multiple times, then tie it all together so that it flows from start to finish.

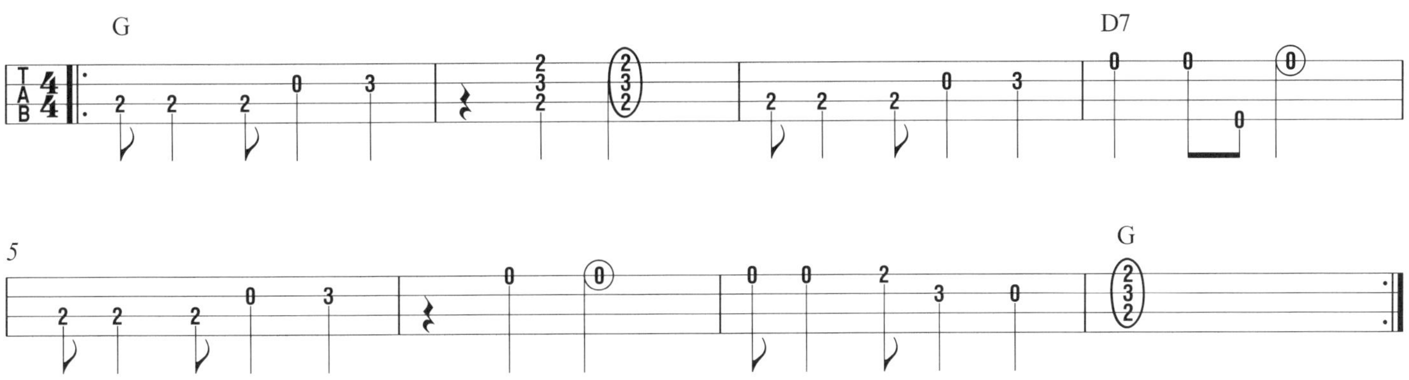

DRUNKEN SAILOR

Now let's try a timeless, two-chord sea shanty, brushing the Em chord alongside melody and droning.

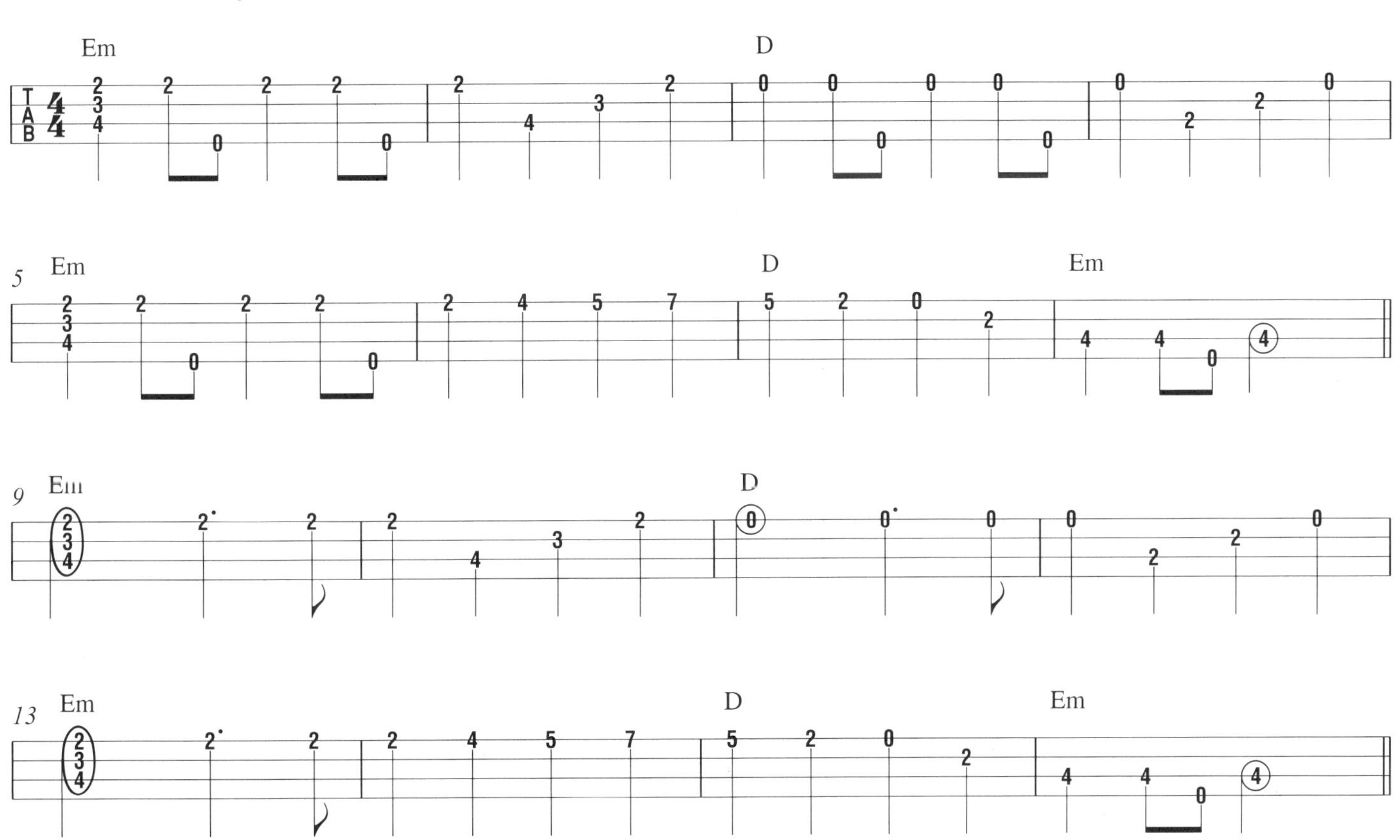

PLAYING SCALES WITH CLAWHAMMER

SCALES IN C

To start, we'll be playing the C major scale with added drones. Watch and listen to the video. Try to play it while counting "1 and, 2 and, 3 and, 4 and" for each measure.

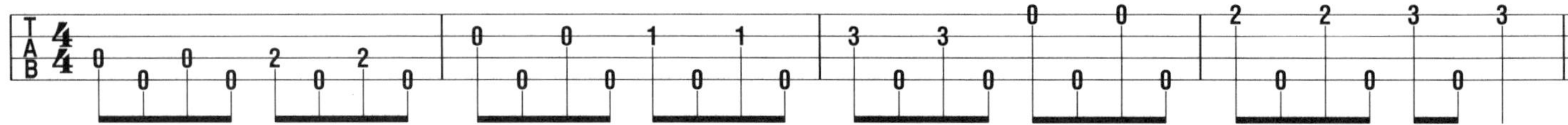

Great Job! Now, let's explore the basic C *blues scale*. Many of these "blue notes" often appear in mountain music (flatted 3rds, 5ths, and 7ths) and give that high, lonesome sound its haunting quality. Count "1, 2, 3, 4" per measure.

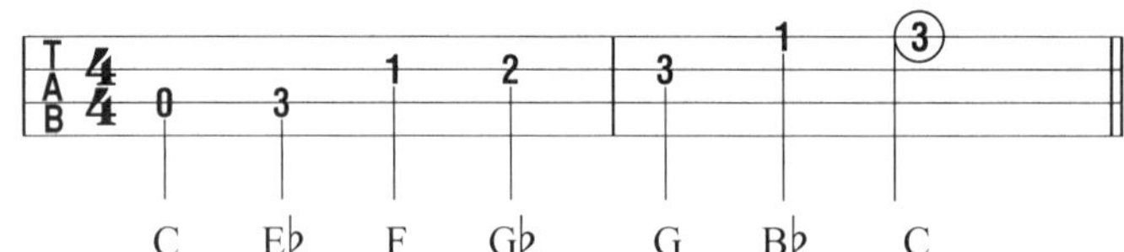

REUBEN'S TRAIN

"Reuben's Train" is a classic bluegrass and old-time tune that is often played on the banjo and fiddle. It features a bluesy sound with the use of the B♭ note (flatted 7th). We can get a bluesy sound when we draw notes from the blues scale, as shown above.

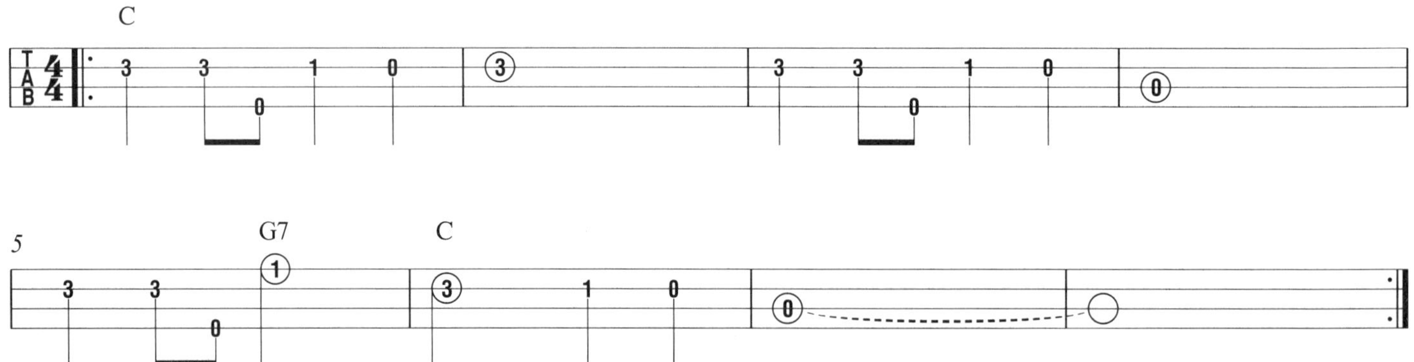

Clawhammer Blues

To hear some great examples of bluesy clawhammer playing, listen to the late, legendary Roscoe Holcomb, Dock Boggs, Tommy Jarrell, and guitarist John Jackson's banjo playing.

BRUSHING CHORDS WITH MELODY AND DRONE

SHADY GROVE

"Shady Grove" is a standard folk and bluegrass song that has its origins in the Irish ballad "Matty Groves." It's a late 18th-century Appalachian chestnut that's been recorded hundreds of times by folks like Doc Watson and even Jerry Garcia of the Grateful Dead.

The goal of the two versions below is to teach you to move seamlessly between playing single-note melody and brushing the occasional E minor chord. When you can do these two things, then you're really starting to get the hang of playing clawhammer.

Brush the E minor chord on the first beat of measure 4.

Shady Grove (Low Version)

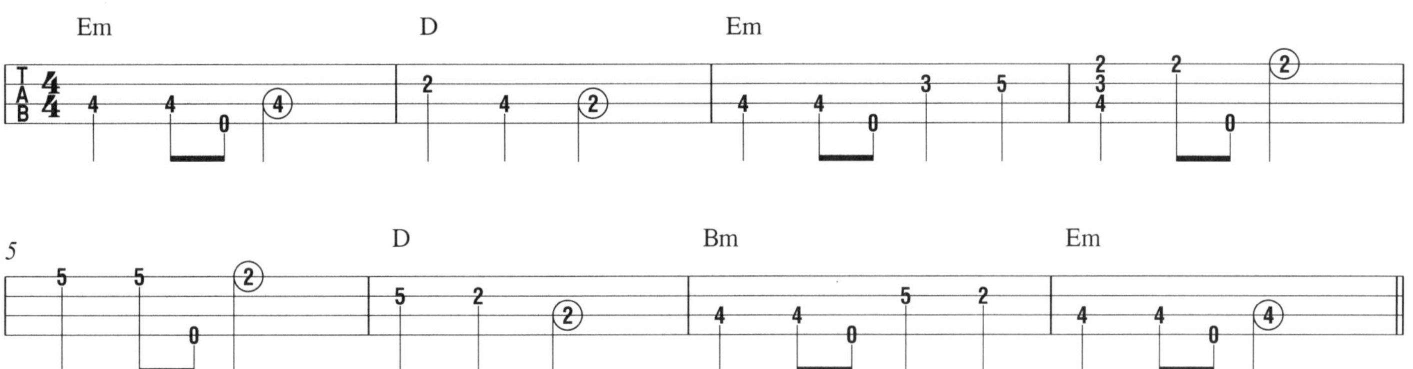

Here's another version of the same tune played up the neck. Brush the E minor chord on the first beat of measure 8.

Shady Grove (High Version)

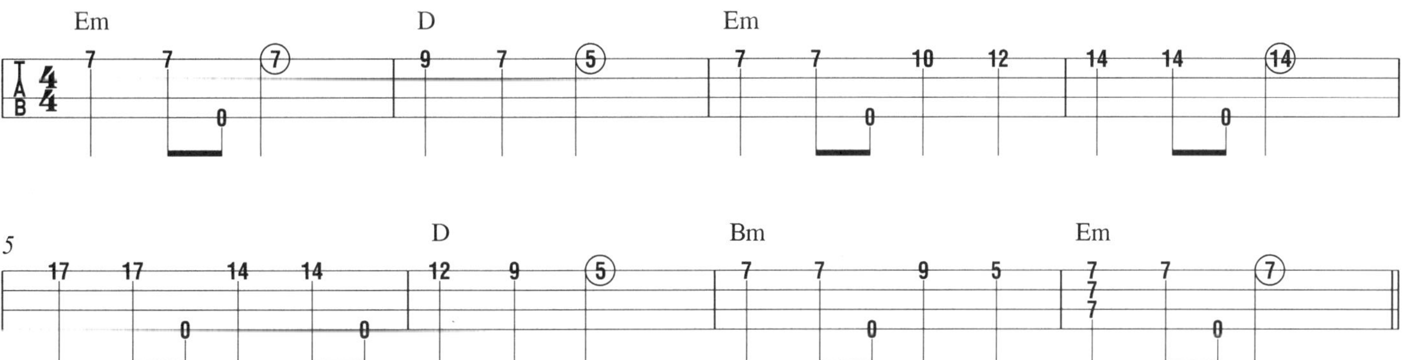

Parking Lot Picker Alert!

"Shady Grove" is one of those tunes that you can always expect to turn up at a bluegrass jam session. It's typically played in the key of A minor, E minor, or D minor. If you want to hear some really sweet versions of this tune, check out recordings or YouTube videos by Ricky Skaggs, Taj Mahal, the Kingston Trio, and Billy Strings.

ADDING SLIDES/SLURS

Sliding between two notes (also referred to as *slurring*) means that the first note is struck and then slid up or down the same string to another note that is **not** struck. There is no separation between the two. For example, if you are sliding from the note B♭ on the 1st fret of the A string to the note B on the 2nd fret of the A string, you'd strike the B♭ once, and then slide your fretting finger up the string to the next note, allowing it to ring out without striking it a second time.

This technique is used often in banjo circles and becomes even more pronounced in the fretless banjo tradition. Listen to some of the best contemporary banjo players today, like Cathy Fink, Stephen Wade, Bruce Molsky, and Walt Koken, to name a few, and you'll hear all of them using this cool technique.

SLIDING EXERCISES

Ukulele players can apply this same technique to their own approach to playing clawhammer. The following exercises are designed to teach you how to use the slide in a song. You'll see two symbols used in the tablature to indicate a slide: The *slide* itself, which is the diagonal line between the two tab numbers, and the *slur*, which is the curved symbol arching over the two notes.

For the first exercise, the slides are played as *grace notes*, which have no rhythmic value. So the B♭ notes on fret 1 are immediately slid into the B notes on fret 2. Watch and listen to the video.

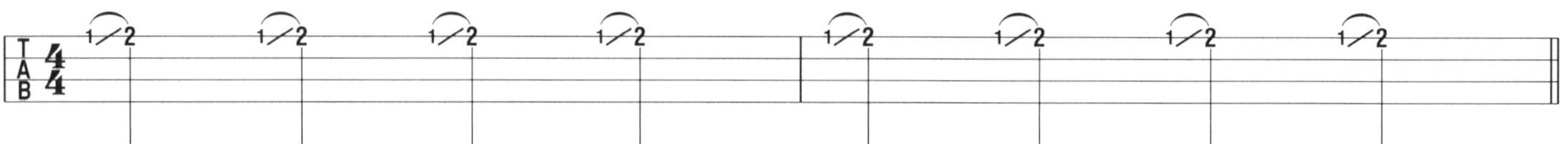

Next, the slides are played more rhythmically, this time using triplets. Slide from fret 1 to fret 2, then strike the D note on the 5th fret of the same string for a "1-2-3" feel. Count "1-2-3, 1-2-3, 1-2-3, 1-2-3," or four triplets per measure.

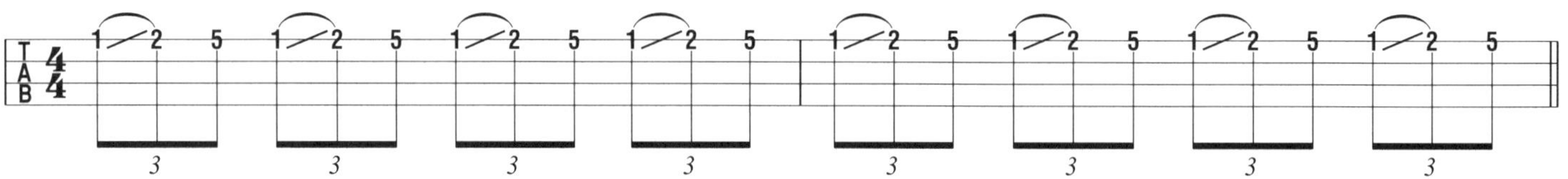

Using a descending G major scale, this exercise includes a new type of slide, sometimes called a "slide from nowhere." This is similar to the grace-note slide above, where you immediately slide into the note. The difference here is that you can start your slide from any lower point on the same string as your destination note, and not from a specific note or fret. Check out the video to see this in action!

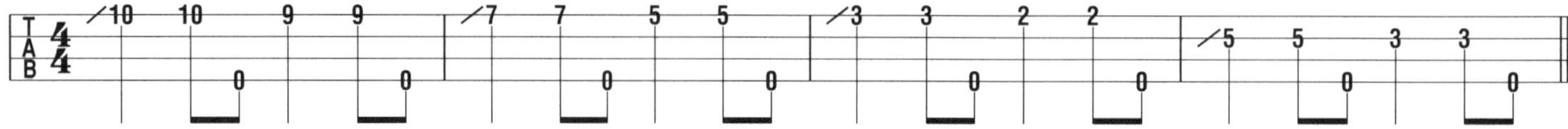

The last slide exercise combines slides and drones.

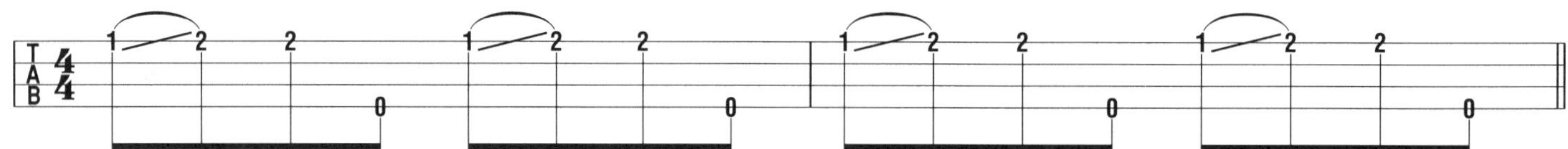

SKILLET GOOD AND GREASY

"Skillet Good and Greasy" is an early country favorite, popular with string-band musicians and pre-war bluesmen. Possibly dating back as far as the late 1800s, this song is also reminiscent of a few other common folk variants, like the Mississippi John Hurt song, "Pay Day." The main slides in our arrangement go from the blue note, B♭ (or the flat 3rd), to the B natural on the 2nd fret of the A string, giving this a cool, bluesy sound. Listen to versions of this tune by Uncle Dave Macon of early Grand Old Opry fame and bluesman Moses Rascoe.

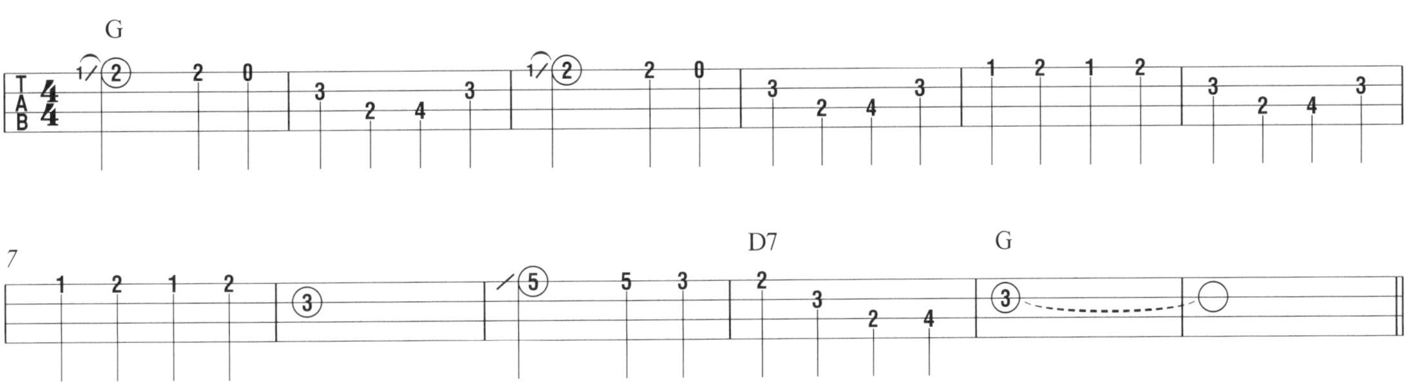

Lil' Rev playing clawhammer on his long-neck Pete Seeger-style Vega banjo, circa 2012.
Photo by Alan Friedman.

SCALE REVIEW

In preparation for the next couple of tunes, let's do a quick review of the G major scale as it moves up the neck on the E and A strings. The notes in the scale are G-A-B-C-D-E-F#-G. Count "1, 2, 3, 4" for each four-beat measure.

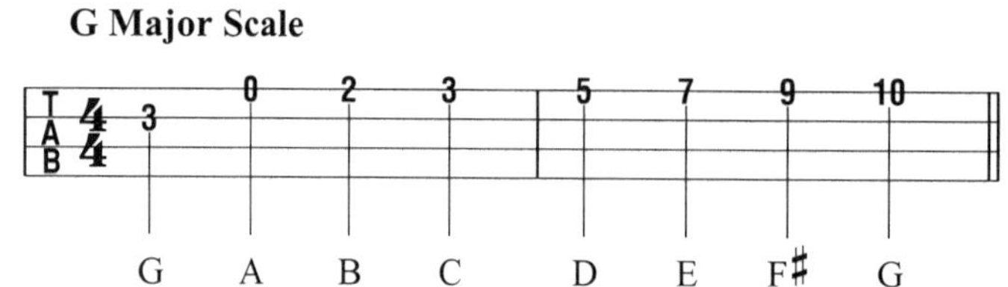

Great job! Now let's look at the G blues scale, which is created when we flat the 3rd and 5th degrees in the major scale, while omitting the 2nd and 6th degrees. First, we'll play it with quarter notes and no drones, counting "1, 2, 3, 4":

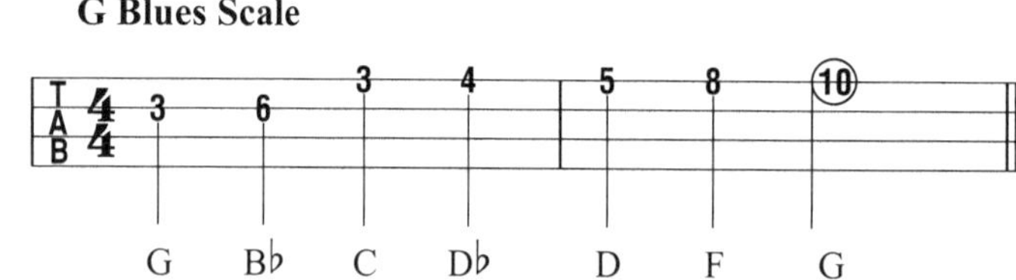

Next, add drones to the scale with the following exercise.

G Blues Scale with Drones

Now you're ready to try the following blues piece, titled "Sliding into the Blues." To play this piece, you'll need to slide into the 2nd-fret B note, followed by a D note on the 5th fret. Then, slide up from the 5th to the 8th fret, finally landing on the E note on the 7th fret. This sequence will repeat in a few different places throughout this 12-bar blues. This not only demonstrates how elements of blues and boogie can be integrated into the clawhammer tradition, but also how we can start to slide into notes up and down the scale.

Sliding into the Blues

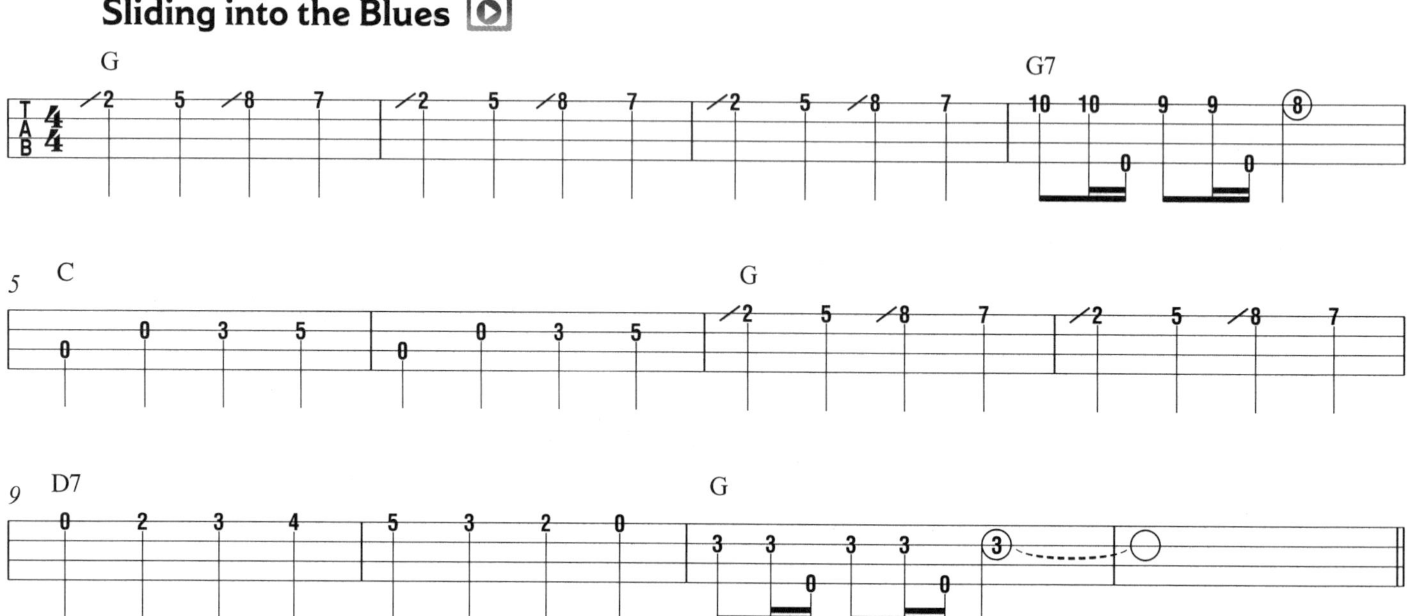

LISTENING TO THE GREAT BANJO PLAYERS

The recorded history of the banjo and its clawhammer proponents provides us with some really enchanting moments in hearing not only its evolution, but also its breadth and enduring nature.

While the ukulele's re-entrant high-G string gives us the tacit ability to play clawhammer, the real source of our inspiration will always come from the banjo itself. Thus, it behooves us to spend some quality time soaking up the music of clawhammerers past and present. Taking the time to really let it sink in will help you develop a better sense of the fundamentals, as well as an appreciation for the rich history that you have now become a part of. Below is a list of some of my favorite clawhammer banjo recordings; some of these are classic in their own right, while others are slightly obscure.

My hope is that this music will inspire you to become a better clawhammer player and hopefully to undertake an interest in its profoundly rich history. The recordings listed below represent a number of different approaches to picking the banjo, including clawhammer, two-finger style, three-finger style, Scruggs style, and melodic clawhammer.

Dock Boggs *Volume 3* (Folkways 3903)

Fleming Brown *Appalachian Banjo Songs & Ballads* (Folk-Legacy CD-4)

Howard Bursen *Cider in the Kitchen* (Folk-Legacy FSI-74)

Cathy Fink with Marcy Marxer *Banjo Talkin'* (Rounder 11661-0599-2)

Béla Fleck and Abigail Washburn (Rounder 11661-36408-01)

Dan Gellert *Waitin' on the Break of Day* (DG 8039)

The Highwoods String Band *Feed Your Babies Onions* (Rounder CD 11569)

Roscoe Holcomb *Close to Home* (Folkways 2374)

Jarrell, Creed, Lineberry & Patterson *June Apple* (Heritage CD-038)

Bruce Molsky and Bob Carlin *Take Me as I Am* (CarTunes 105)

Ken Perlman *Clawhammer Banjo & Fingerstyle Guitar Solos* (Folkways 31098)

Frank Proffitt *Sings Folk Songs* (Folkways 2360)

Ola Belle Reed *Rising Sun Melodies* (Folkways 40202)

Art Rosenbaum *The Iron Mountain Baby* (89211702442)

Flatt & Scruggs *The Complete Mercury Recordings* (Mercury 0000070-02)

Mike Seeger *Southern Banjo Styles* (Folkways 40107)

Pete Seeger *American Favorite Ballads, Volumes 1–5* (Folkways 40155)

Hobart Smith *Blue Ridge Legacy* (Rounder 11661-1799-2)

The Stanley Brothers and the Clinch Mountain Boys
The Complete Mercury Recordings (Mercury 2070229)

Pete Steele *Banjo Tunes and Songs* (Folkways 3828)

Molly Tenenbaum *Instead of a Pony* (7-83707-53142-7)

Stephen Wade *Dancing in the Parlor* (County CD-2721)

Stephen Wade *Dancing Home* (Flying Fish 70543)

Wade Ward *Uncle Wade: A Memorial to Wade Ward* (Folkways 2380)

Compilations with Various Artists:

Altamont: Black Stringband Music from the Library of Congress (Rounder 0238)

American Banjo Tunes & Songs in Scruggs Style (Folkways 2314)

Black Banjo Songsters of North Carolina and Virginia (Folkways 40079)

Old Time Banjo Festival (Rounder 11661-0584-2)

Traditional Music from Grayson and Carroll Counties (Folkways 3811)

Banjo Time (Liza Jane)

Check out this bonus video of me demonstrating the clawhammer technique on the banjo, where it all began!

Pete Seeger's famous banjo head says, "This machine surrounds hate and forces it to surrender."
Photo courtesy of Rik Palieri

LEARNING TO HAMMER ON

A *hammer-on* is one of many fretting-hand techniques used by stringed-instrument players to create more percussion and embellishment when playing a melody. *Hammer-ons* allow you to slur notes together cleanly and quickly without any sound between them. Essentially, after striking the first note, you drop (or "hammer") your fretting-hand finger down onto the second note without actually striking it again.

THE BASIC HAMMER-ON

To start, pluck an open string, like the open C string for example. As soon as you hear it vibrate, let the middle finger of your fretting hand hammer down onto the 2nd fret of the C string (the note D), without striking the string a second time. Count "1 and, 2 and, 3 and, 4 and" in each measure. A slur with the letter "h" over it is used to indicate a hammer-on in the tablature. Please be sure to watch the videos for this and the following exercises to get a visual of how this technique is executed.

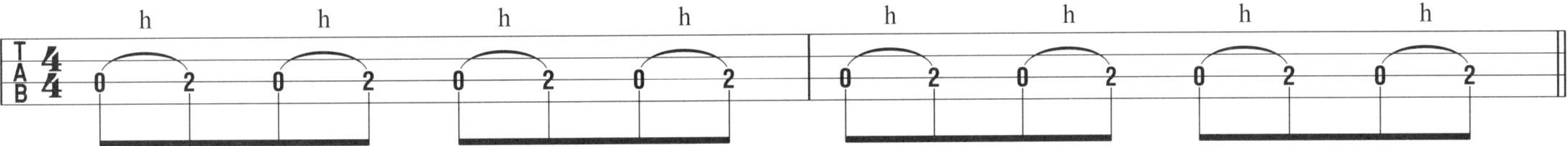

HAMMER-ON EXERCISES

Here are some exercises to help you master this technique.

Using a C *major pentatonic scale* (a five-note scale derived from the major scale), you'll hammer across the open C, E, and A strings to produce the sound of this scale.

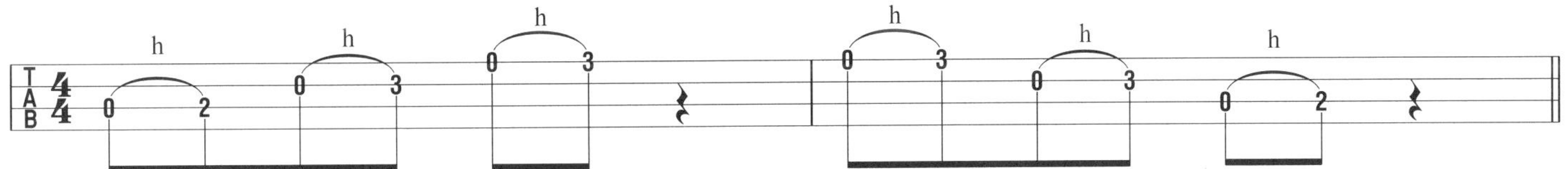

This next exercise is in two parts. The first part will help you perfect combining a hammer-on with a drone, and the second adds a brush stroke to the hammer and drone.

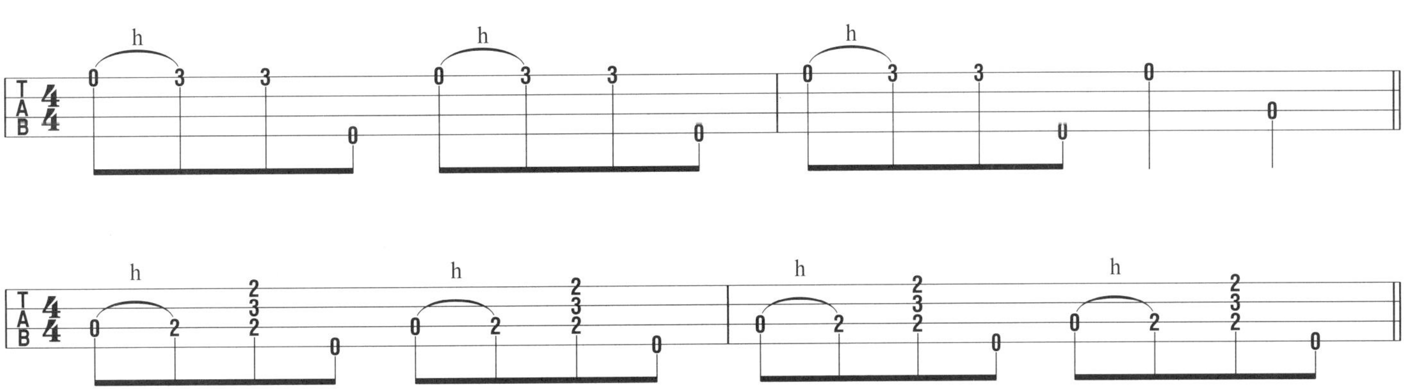

Here's another variation of "Boil 'Em Cabbage Down" to practice hammer-ons.

Hammer 'Em Cabbage Down

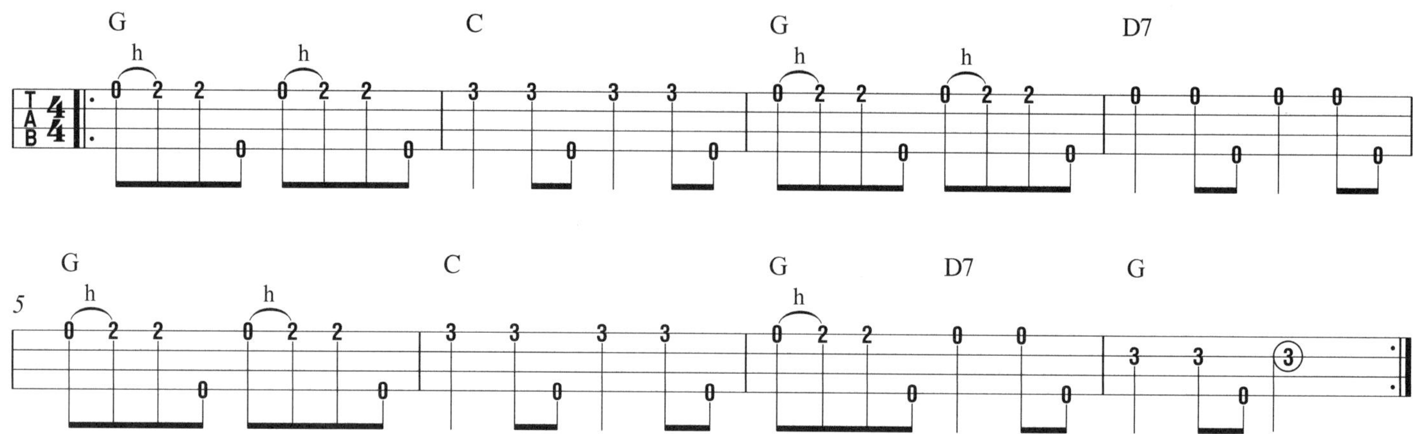

Here's a bluesy exercise that hammers onto the 3rd fret of the C string, which is the note E♭. As touched on earlier, in the key of C this note is what we call a flatted 3rd or "blue note." Blue notes give us that spooky sound that makes playing the blues in a clawhammer style really cool.

Mean Old Hammer-On Blues

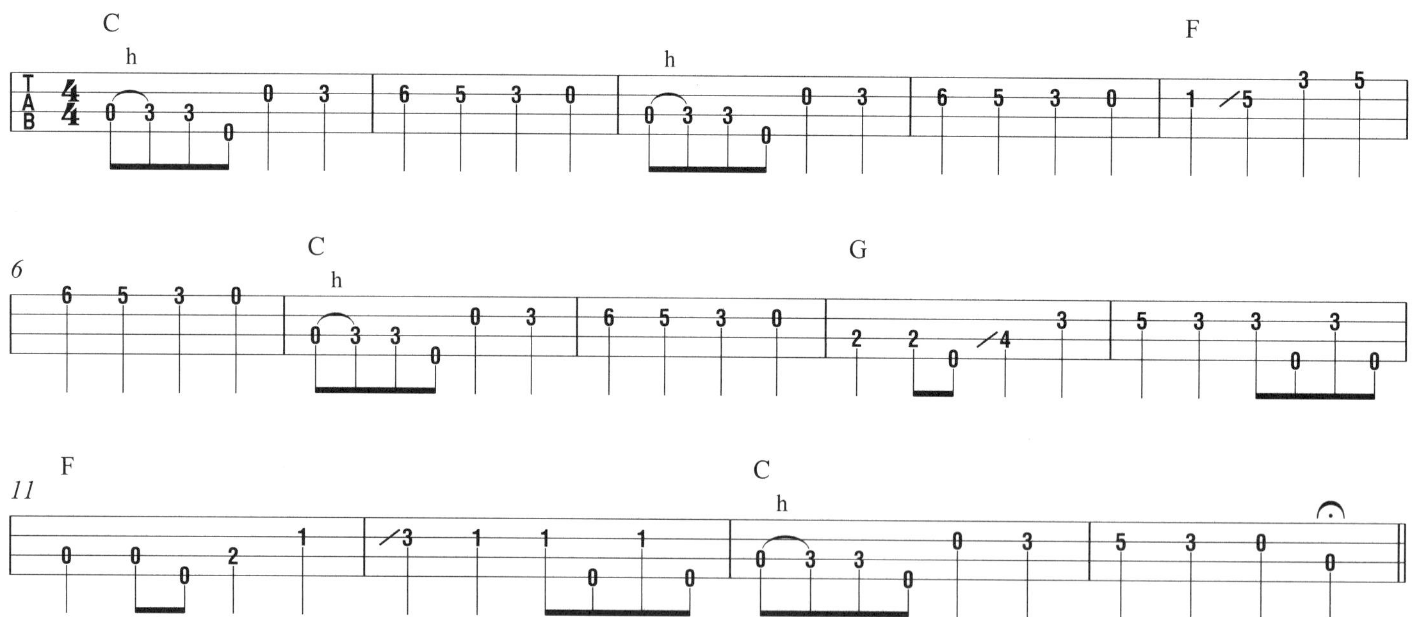

The hammer-on is a technique that needn't be overused. In other words, a little bit goes a very long way. Sometimes, one or two well-placed hammer-ons can really spice up an arrangement.

The following exercise combines a simple 5th- to 7th-fret hammer-on with a slide from the 5th fret down to the 3rd fret, all done on the A string. (It's important to note that slides can move in an ascending or descending direction.) Eventually, you'll learn to combine a variety of different fretting-hand techniques together to create a really effective clawhammer style.

Hammers and Slides

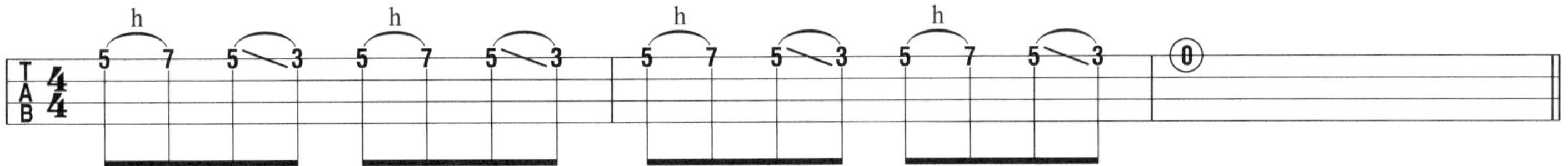

WALKING IN THE PARLOR

"Walking in the Parlor" is an old-time piece that's popular amongst fiddlers and mountain dulcimer players. Usually, it is played in the key of D or G. This is my arrangement in the key of C, which works well with the open ukulele strings. If you want to play it in a more fiddle-friendly key, later on in the book we'll discuss how to re-tune your ukulele or put on a capo so that you can play well with others and be in the same key at your local jam session. Watch out for the hammer-on in the second measure of the B section. You'll hammer from the 5th fret to the 7th, then slide from the 5th fret down to the 3rd fret. You should be ready for this, as it's exactly what you practiced in the previous exercise.

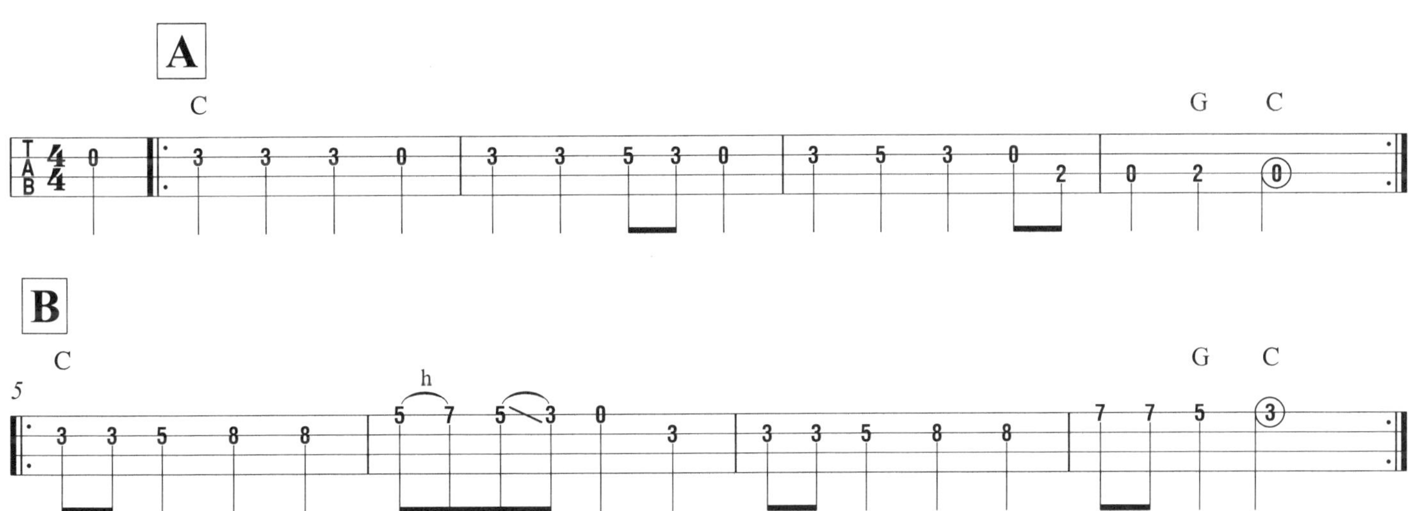

LEARNING TO PULL OFF

I like to think of a *pull-off* as a hammer-on in reverse! Pull-offs can be very useful when playing faster or busier passages that might otherwise be harder to pick. In the tablature, a pull-off looks very similar to a hammer-on, but instead of an "h" above the slur, there is a "p."

THE BASIC PULL-OFF

To start, strike any fretted note. After striking the note, pull your fretting finger off of it, allowing the next fretted note (or open string) to sound. The transition between the notes of the pull-off should be smooth and seamless. Just like executing a hammer-on, the first note is struck and the second note isn't. For this exercise, count "1 and, 2 and, 3 and, 4 and" for each bar. Remember to strike the first note and pull off to the second.

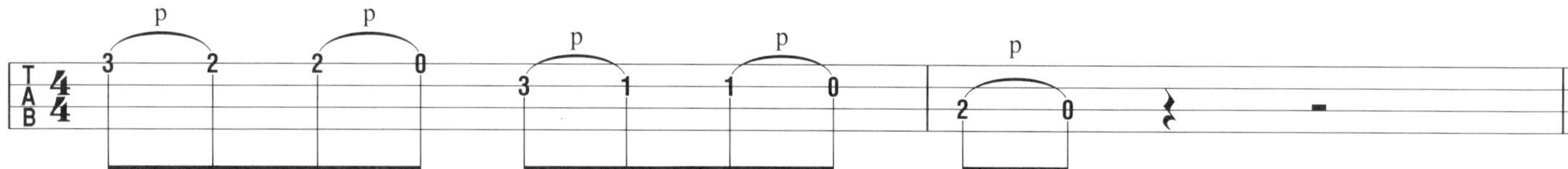

Thanks to old-time musician Gail Heil of Spring Grove, MN, who taught me how to play the clawhammer stroke.
Photo courtesy of Bob Bovee.

PULL-OFF EXERCISES

Here's a variety of exercises geared towards helping you become more proficient at pull-offs. Once you're comfortable with pull-offs, we can begin to combine them with slides and hammer-ons for some really tasty clawhammer BBQ!

For the first exercise, fret the D note (C string, 2nd fret) and gently pull the string downwards to sound the open-string C note. Repeat as desired. Count "1 and, 2 and, 3 and, 4 and" in each measure.

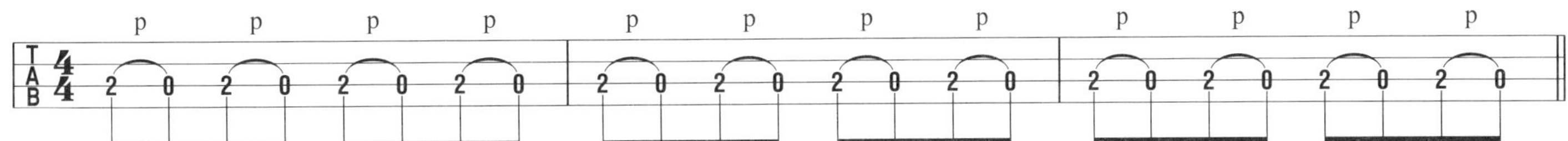

You played the C major pentatonic scale earlier—a five-note scale (C-D-E-G-A) that is commonly used in pop, rock, country, and folk music. The C major pentatonic scale is a lot like a C major scale, but with the 4th and 7th degrees (F and B) removed. Remember, only strike the first note, and let the second one ring out without striking it again.

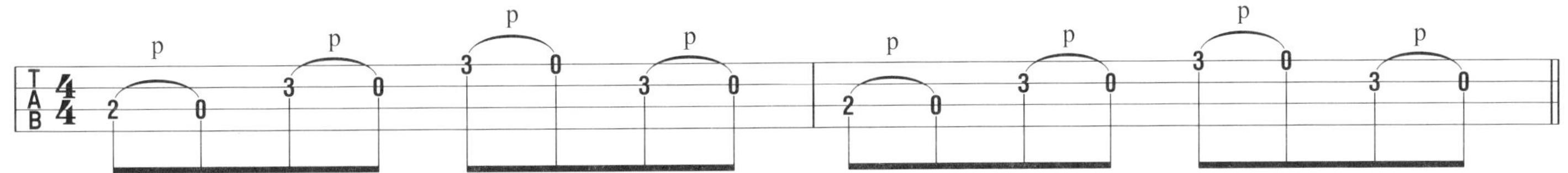

The next exercise demonstrates how you can pull-off more than one note. Strike the G note (3rd fret, E string) and pull-off to the 1st fret (F note), followed by the open E string. In sequence, your fretting-hand ring finger on the note G pulls off to your index finger on the F, which then pulls off to the open-string E.

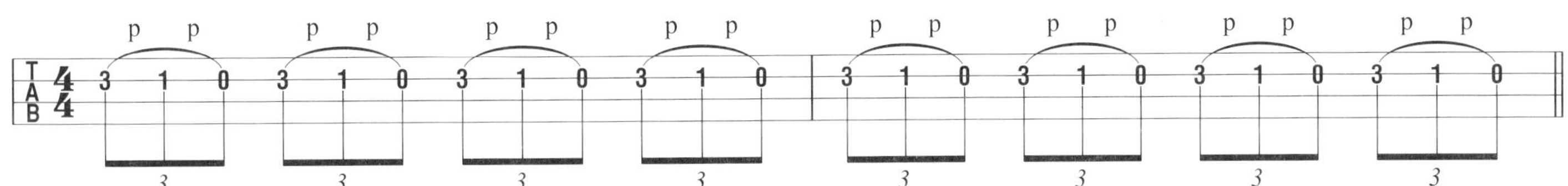

Here is the basic melody of "Twinkle, Twinkle Little Star" with a pull-off towards the end of the phrase.

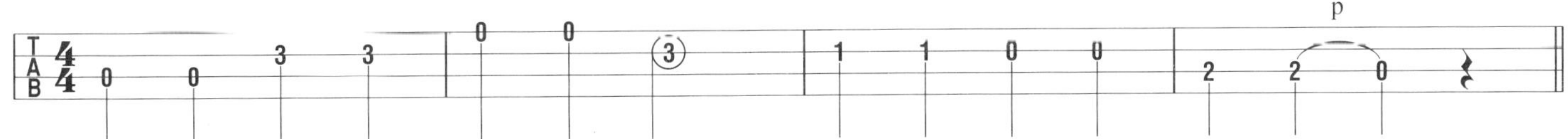

COMBINING TECHNIQUES WITH PULL-OFFS

The following exercises combine pull-offs with some of the other techniques you've learned. The first exercise adds a chordal brush and drone. Count "1 and, 2 and, 3 and, 4 and" for each measure.

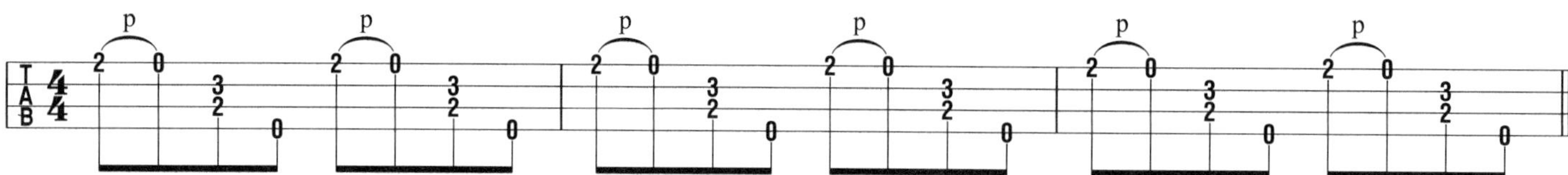

Here's a cool example that alternates between hammer-ons and pull-offs:

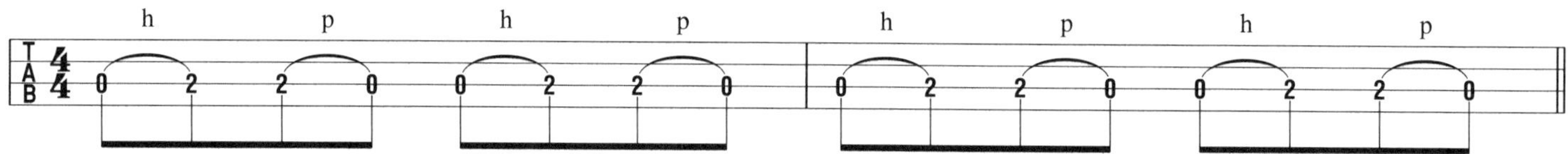

Here's the old American folk song "Paw Paw Patch" that's fun to play with some added pull-offs. Watch and listen to the video example to see and hear how this one is done.

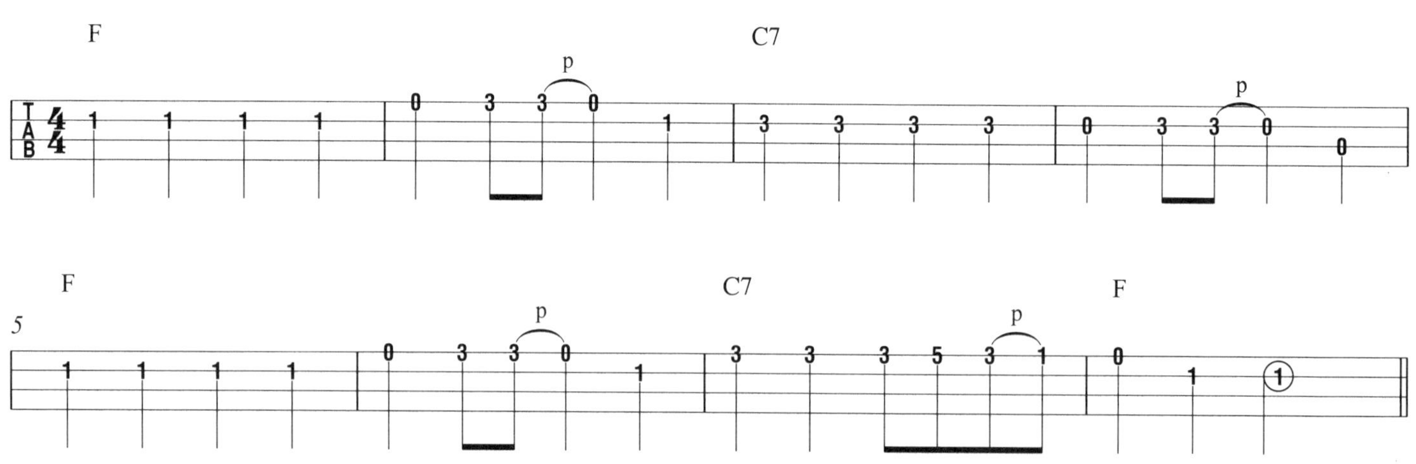

The last exercise is a great way to familiarize yourself with the G major scale while also integrating hammer-ons and pull-offs.

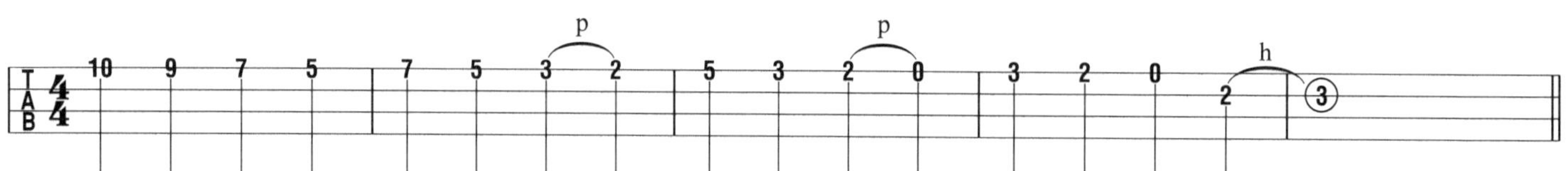

SANDY BOYS

"Sandy Boys" was thought to be a favorite song of the legendary old-time fiddler Edden Hammons, of the famous Hammons family. Edden lived from 1875 to 1955 in Webster County, West Virginia, and was regarded as one of the state's finest fiddlers, having won many fiddle contests over the course of his life. Interestingly, he made his living by hunting, fishing, moonshining, and fiddling most of his adult life.

Clawhammer banjo player Dan Levenson told me that the tune first appeared in print in *Phil Rice's Correct Method for the Banjo* (1858), titled "Sandy Boy."

"Sandy Boys" has a few simple pull-offs as well as some basic droning. It's often played at a moderate tempo, and due to its modal nature, sounds dynamite when played in a clawhammer style. Watch and listen to the video a few times to absorb the sound and rhythmic flavor of this cool piece before taking a stab at it, and remember that each part is played twice.

A Note About Tunings and Keys

If you're playing "Sandy Boys" solo in a ukulele setting, then C is a great key as it utilizes lots of open strings and sounds really cool. If you'd like to play this arrangement with others in a bluegrass or old-time setting, you'll want to consider putting a capo on the 2nd fret or re-tuning your ukulele up one whole step to A-D-F♯-B (D6 tuning, or "D tuning"). In both instances, you'll be in the fiddle-friendly key of D.

While the key of D is a fiddle- and banjo-friendly key, "Sandy Boys" is usually played in the key of A and you're liable to send some folks reeling (no pun intended!) if you bust this out in the key of D or C. This is all to say "beware," as there's a difference between uke-friendly keys and the banjo/fiddle's traditionally favored keys.

PLAYING TUNES WITH COMBINED TECHNIQUES

SAIL AWAY LADIES

Song Explanation

"Sail Away Ladies" is another standard in old-time repertoire and a favorite amongst clawhammer players across North America. The tune is often associated with Uncle Dave Macon of early Grand Old Opry fame, though its origins can be traced back to the late 1800s. This arrangement will take some repetition in order to integrate all three of the left-hand techniques into one seamless piece—slides, hammer-ons, and pull-offs. Once you've put in the time, it's loads of fun to jam this tune with other musicians.

A helpful practice hint is to learn the accompaniment or backup first by playing along with the video, and then learn and master the melody. This way, you'll be ready to perform both the melody and backup, taking turns and allowing others to play the lead while you switch to rhythm. Another approach is to use your smartphone or recording device to record the backing track, and then play along with yourself by playing the melody, making sure not to slow down or get ahead of yourself. Lastly, it's a good idea to practice these tunes with a metronome; start slowly at 60–70 bpm (beats per minute) and work up to 90–100 bpm. This will prepare you to play melodies like this at a variety of different tempos.

Song Performance

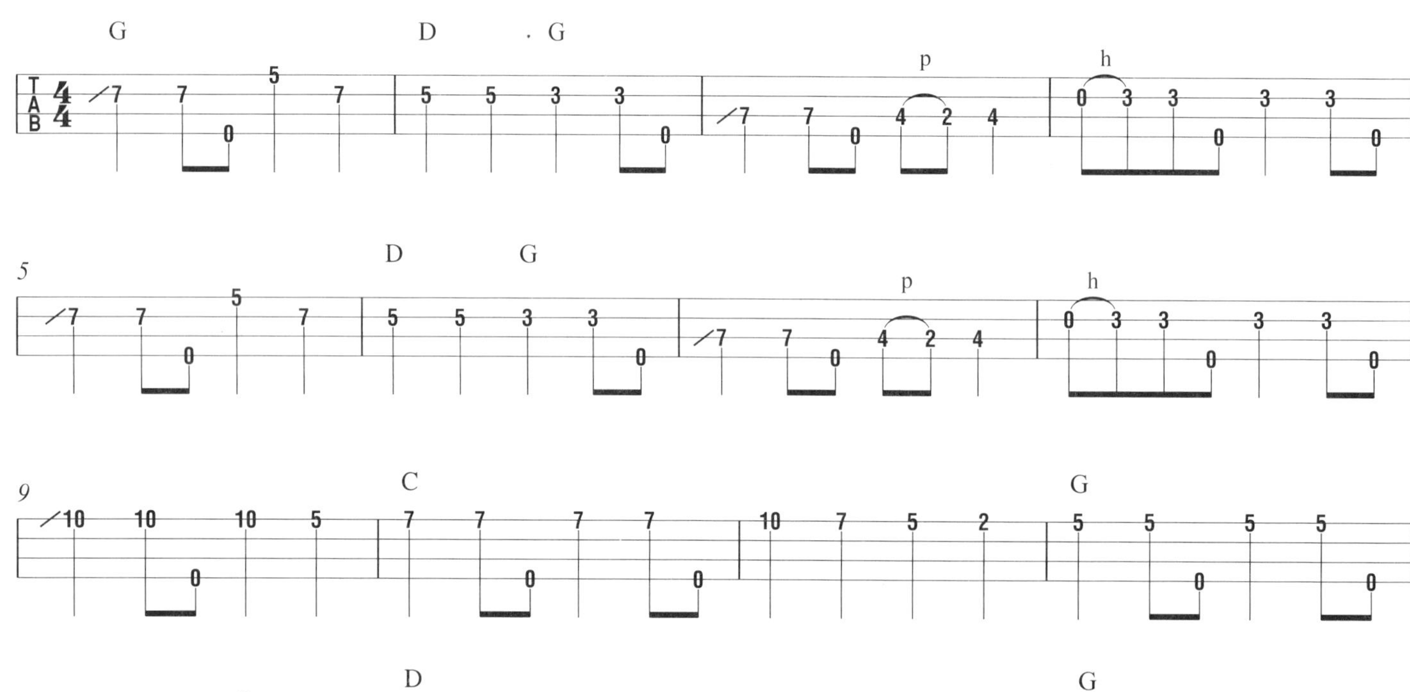

Lyrics:

If ever I get my new house done,
Sail away ladies, sail away.
Give my old one to my son.

Sail away ladies, sail away.
Don't you rock 'em, di-dee-o. (3x)
Sail away ladies, sail away.

BARLOW KNIFE

Song Explanation

Here's another jam standard called "Barlow Knife" that's a three-part tune arranged in the key of G.

The A section combines hammer-on and pull-off techniques without the use of drones, and then moves into the B section with slides and pull-offs. The C section is comprised of slides, pull-offs, and hammer-ons, as well as some very basic droning.

To prepare you for this arrangement, we'll begin with three warm-up exercises, followed by the full song.

Hammer-On Warm-Up

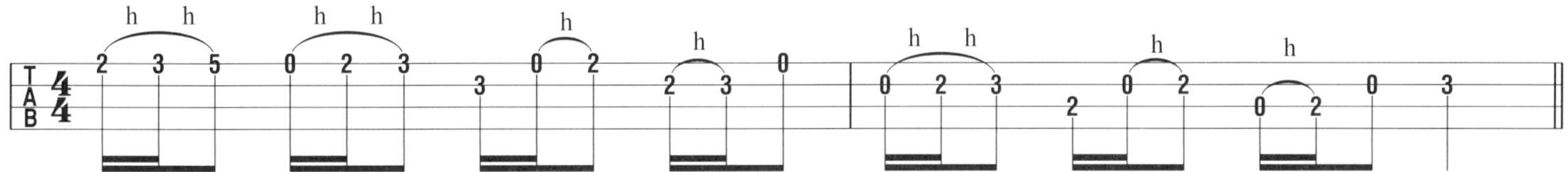

Pull-Off Warm-Up

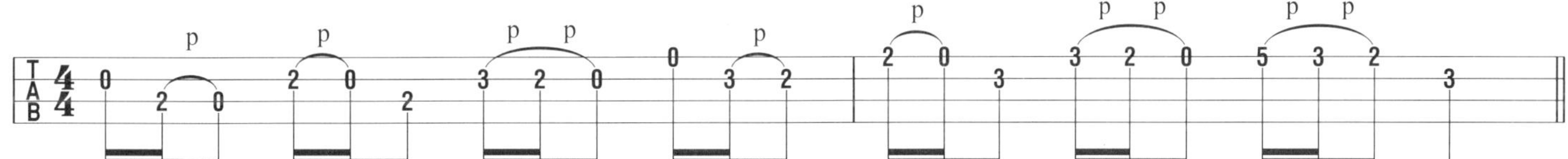

Slide Warm-Up

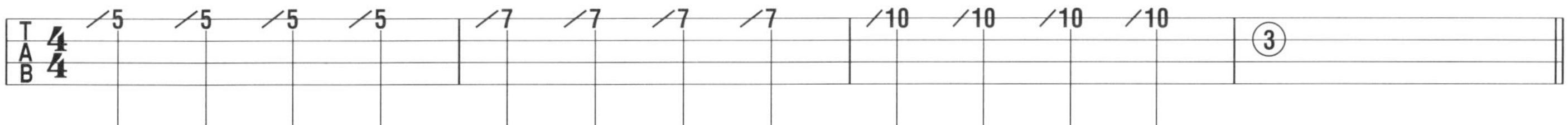

Barlow Knife

Song Performance

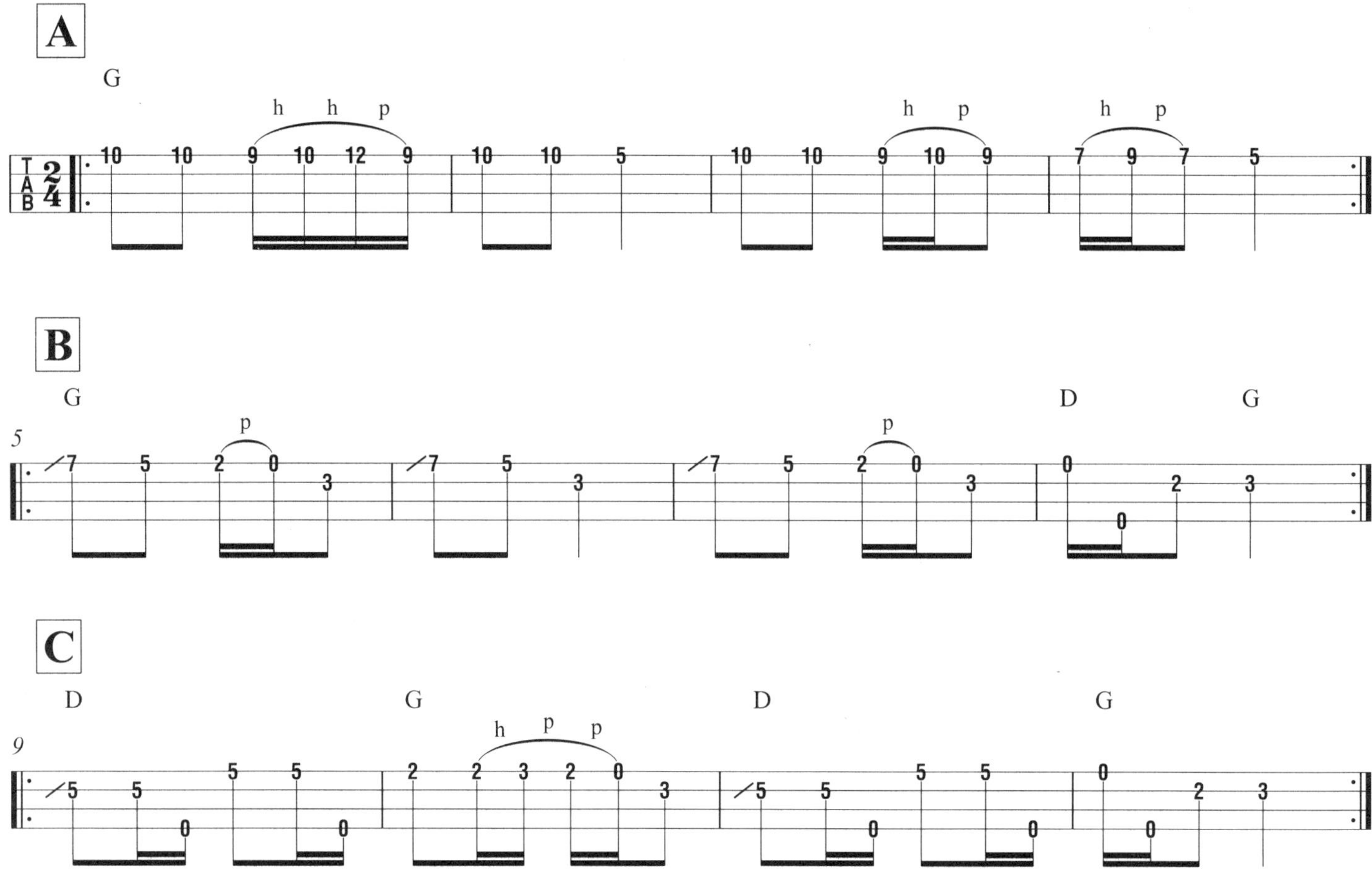

One of Lil' Rev's favorite clawhammer players is Dan Levenson. Dan is a tireless educator, historian, and clawhammer banjo guru. You can catch Dan at old-time music gatherings across the country. Photo courtesy of Steve Meckler.

ON THE ROAD TO BOSTON

Song Explanation

"On the Road to Boston" dates back to the American Revolutionary War era. It is thought to have been played as a fife and drum melody, and is sometimes called "Nathanael Greene's March," named after the famed Major-General Nathanael Greene. Greene served under George Washington during the Boston campaign, among others, and was thought to be Washington's most trusted general.

This catchy piece is very easy to play with some simple pull-offs in both the A and B sections. Review the video a few times and let the tune sink in a bit before trying out this arrangement.

A Note About Tunings and Keys

I have arranged "On the Road to Boston" in the uke-friendly key of C, but you can easily adapt this to the key of D by putting a capo on the 2nd fret or re-tuning the ukulele up a whole step to A-D-F#-B. Both options will put this arrangement in the key of D, where banjos, fiddles, and dulcimers will be more welcoming whence you call out this tune at the next old-time jam!

Song Performance

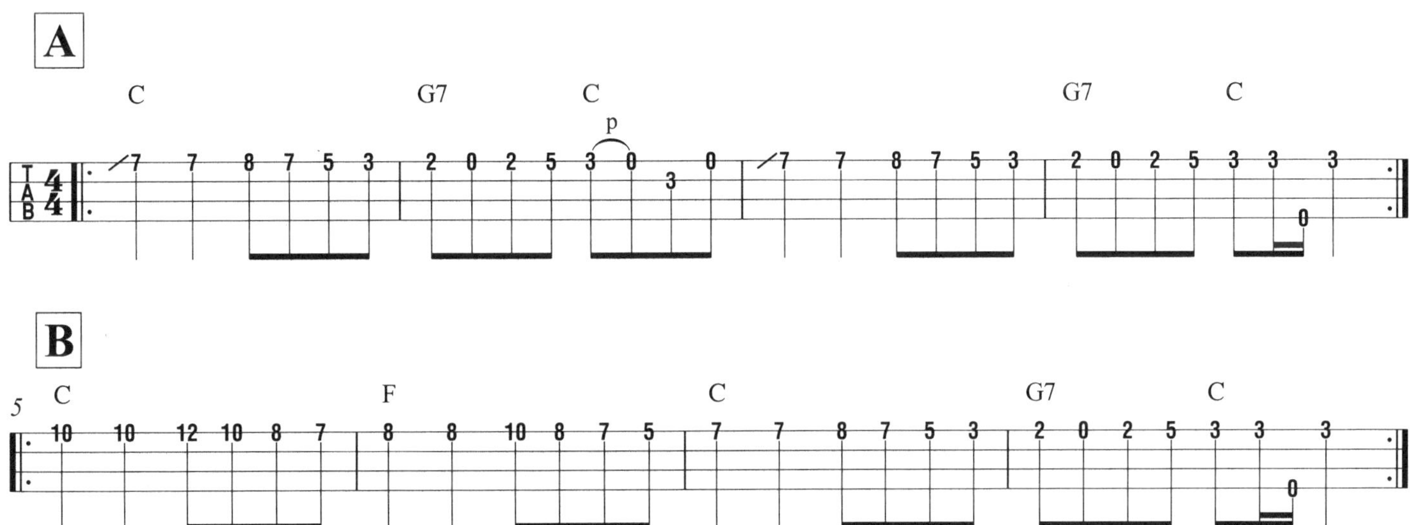

OLD MOLLY HARE

Song Explanation

The next arrangement is a standard, old-timey piece that you'll often hear played in A, D, or G. "Old Molly Hare" is fun, easy, and highly infectious. There's an infinite number of possibilities for variations and it lays down great in the key of G using the high-G string on the ukulele to keep the drone going. The third and fourth measures of both sections contain some fun pull-offs and hammer-ons to try out.

Make note of the chord changes above the melody line and practice using a "boom-chuck" strum to accompany this piece. Remember, it's just as important to know the backup as it is to know the melody. Record yourself playing the accompaniment, then try playing along or simply play along with the video to this lesson.

Song Performance

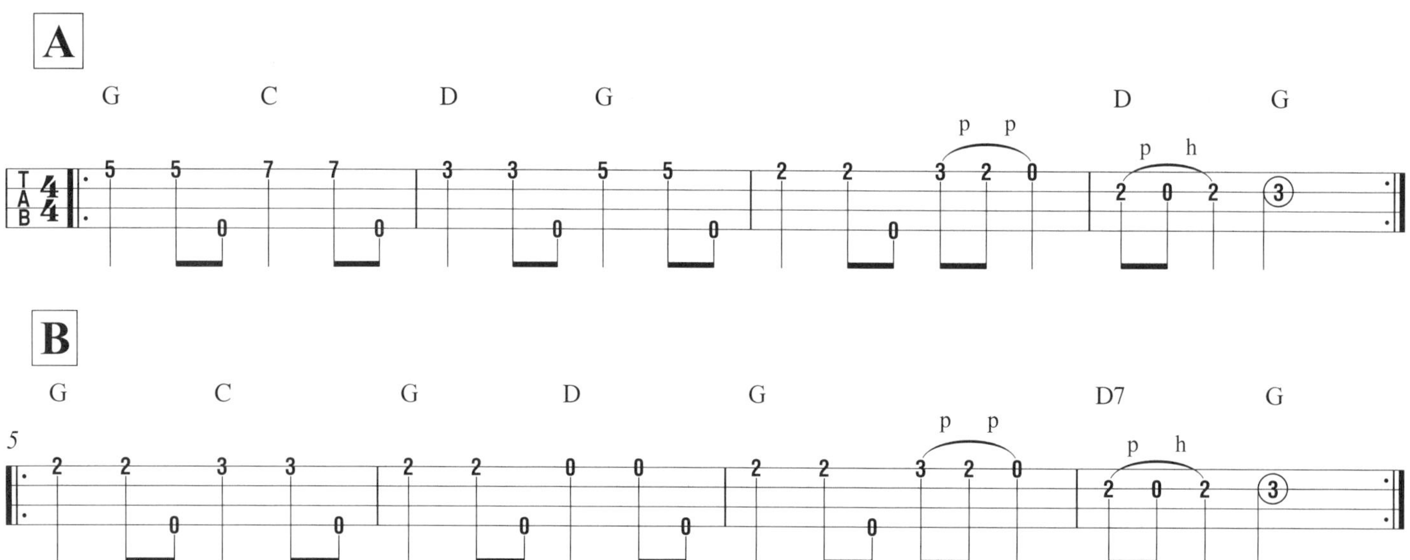

Beansprout luthier and clawhammer ukulele guru Aaron Keim at home in his workshop in Hood River, OR. Aaron builds dynamite banjo ukuleles, baritones, and all sorts of ukes! Photo courtesy of Aaron Keim.

CRIPPLE CREEK

Song Explanation

"Cripple Creek" is a very popular fiddle tune that's a real chestnut in the bluegrass community. This tune is just pure fun to play! What's great about this arrangement is that it combines single-note melody with chords, drones, slides, hammer-ons, and pull-offs, making this a really great example of a tune that contains all of the techniques we've previously worked on.

Be sure to hold down an A chord in the first measure so the drone note is played with the 2nd fret of the G string (an A note). In the second measure, be ready to hammer-on from the D note to the E note, or the 2nd fret to the 4th fret on the C string. Also, be aware that at the end of every section, you'll be brushing twice on the E7 chord and then once on the A chord. In the B section, the first note is a grace note, sliding from the 2nd fret to the 4th fret on the A string (from B to C♯), followed by a pull-off from B to A.

There's a lot of repetition in this tune, so once you've put in a little time, you'll love how easy this piece is to play. To hear other cool versions of "Cripple Creek," listen to Lil' Rev play it on his 2009 album *Drop Baby Drop*. Also check out bluegrass legends Flatt & Scruggs' version on YouTube.

Song Performance

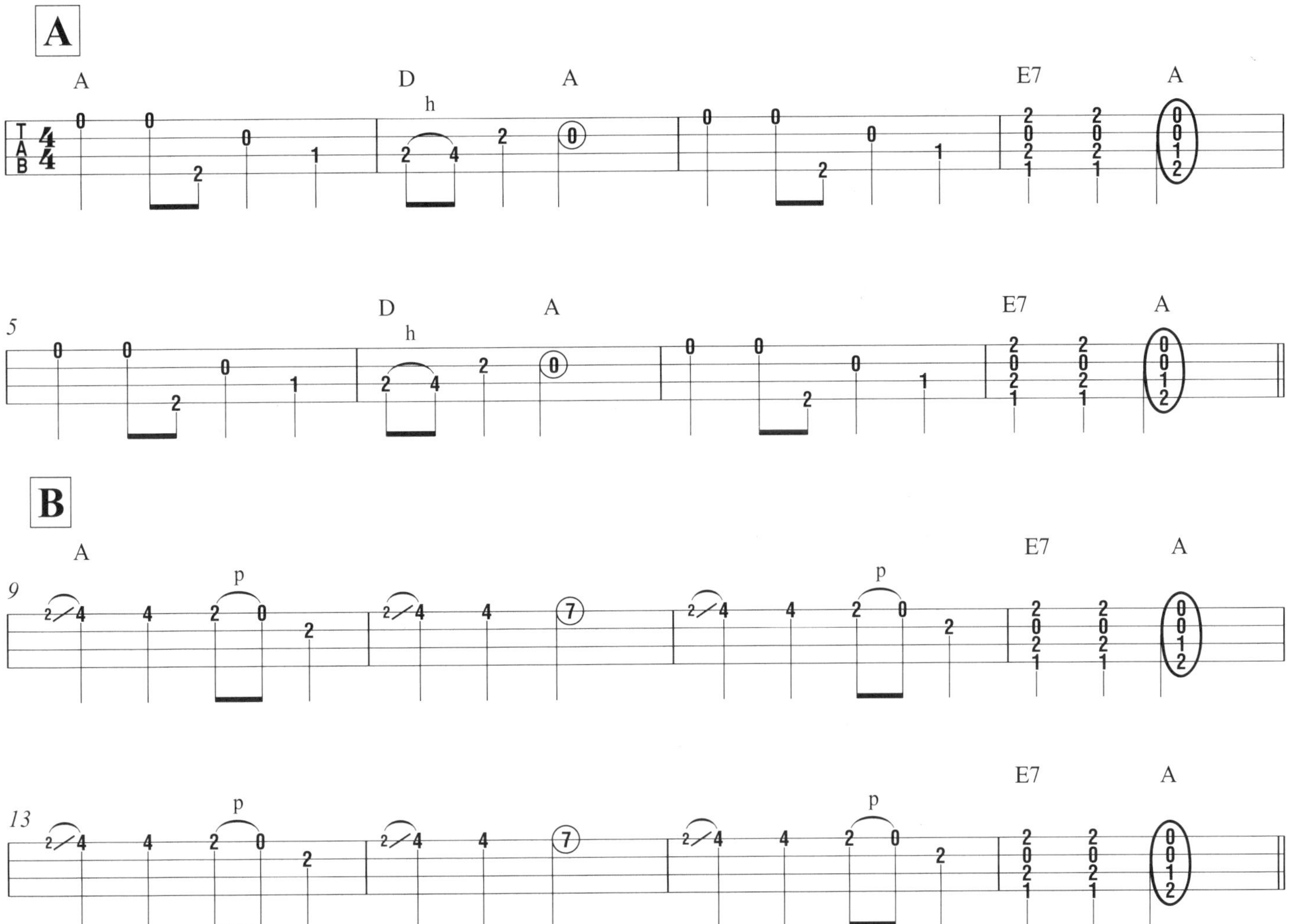

THE ART OF RE-TUNING THE UKULELE

Earlier in the book, we began discussing the concept of re-tuning the ukulele from standard C tuning (GCEA) to D tuning (ADF#B), as well as other alternatives. The reality is that there are a lot of folks who might enjoy learning to play clawhammer, but don't want to re-tune their instruments. Thus, there's a conundrum of whether to arrange tunes in the more uke-friendly keys of C and F versus the fiddle- and banjo-friendly keys of D and G.

If one is going to play solo or isn't necessarily planning to join a jam, then playing a tune like "Arkansas Traveler" in C using C tuning isn't a problem; it sounds great, lays down well with the use of open strings, and it's just fun to play. The problem occurs when the ukulele player takes his or her C version of a tune to a bluegrass jam, old-time contra dance, or song circle where everyone else knows the tune in its common key of D. The ukulele player must then think quickly and decide how he or she wants to join the group by playing the tune in D. To do this, he or she can either re-tune the ukulele up to D tuning, or put a capo on the 2nd fret, which raises all the strings up one whole step. The same could be said for songs in the uke-friendly key of F versus the banjo- and fiddle-friendly keys of G or A. This is why I ask all of my students to give D tuning a fair shake and see if they like the brightness of the higher-pitched tuning, both for strumming and picking melodies.

If you own more than one ukulele, one idea that might help you get used to using D tuning is to keep one uke in C tuning and another one in D tuning. This will make things a little less of a hassle in terms of having to re-tune all of the time.

HOW TO RE-TUNE TO D TUNING: A-D-F#-B

Using a tuner or a pitch pipe...

1. Tune the G string (4th string) up one whole step, from G to A.
2. Tune your C string (3rd string) up one whole step, from C to D.
3. Tune your E string (2nd string) up one whole step, from E to F#.
4. Tune your A string (1st string) up one whole step, from A to B.

D tuning was very popular in the vaudeville years, often favored for its punchy brightness. It is still the favored tuning of ukulele players in Canada and a few other parts of the world. So do yourself a big favor and give this time-honored tuning a fair shake!

TUNINGS TO EXPLORE

This book focuses primarily on C and D tuning. However, many of you will be curious about the possibilities that re-tuning offers. Alternate tunings can offer an extremely exciting array of possibilities, and there are many common tunings that clawhammer players like to use.

Before I get into what those possibilities are, it's important to note that both banjo and fiddle players use a variety of different tunings when playing old-time and bluegrass repertoire. In fact, there are some songs that are so unique they have their own tuning... in other words, they're proprietary! Because clawhammer ukulele styles are heavily influenced by fiddle and banjo, we would be missing out if we didn't at least experiment a tad with different tunings, and I encourage you to do so!

Open C Tuning: G–C–E–G

This is a great tuning for blues, slide playing, and less common fiddle tunes in the key of C. Plus, it's super easy to re-tune to—you only have to change one string!

- Tune your A string (1st string) down one whole step to G.

Open G Tuning: G–B–D–G

This is a dynamite open tuning for fiddle tunes, rags, blues, slide playing, and clawhammer pieces in the key of G. You'll need to re-tune three strings for this tuning.

1. Start by tuning the C string (3rd string) down one half step, from C to B.
2. Next, tune your E string (2nd string) down one whole step, from E to D.
3. Lastly, tune your A string (1st string) down one whole step from A to G.

Other Alternate Tuning Options

Here are some other options for re-tuning your ukulele:

Open D Tuning: A–D–F♯–A

This is a great tuning for slide playing, fiddle tunes, fingerpicking, and more.

Open A Tuning: A–C♯–E–A

Here's a fun tuning to try out for tunes in the key of A, like "Devil's Dream."

Mountain Modal: G–C–E♭–G

This banjo-inspired tuning is moved to the ukulele for modal pieces like "June Apple."

Open Gm Tuning: G–B♭–D–G

This is a great tuning for minor-key pieces with access to the G drone for clawhammer, and killer for slide playing!

Open Cm Tuning: G–C–E♭–G

This is the perfect tuning for minor songs and ballads.

PLAYING SONGS IN D TUNING (A–D–F♯–B)

GROUND HOG

"Ground Hog" is a traditional Appalachian folk song. I first heard this performed by flatpicking guitar guru Doc Watson and later discovered a cool, early 78 rpm version by Jack Reedy and His Walker Mountain String Band on the Brunswick Records label that was recorded in February of 1928 in Ashland, Kentucky. Today, this song is most commonly done in mountain dulcimer and banjo circles and makes for a wonderfully easy tune to play in a clawhammer style while in D tuning.

This is a pretty straightforward tune with a melody that lays down well on just two strings with some added droning. Check out the accompanying video as well as the many recorded samples on the internet.

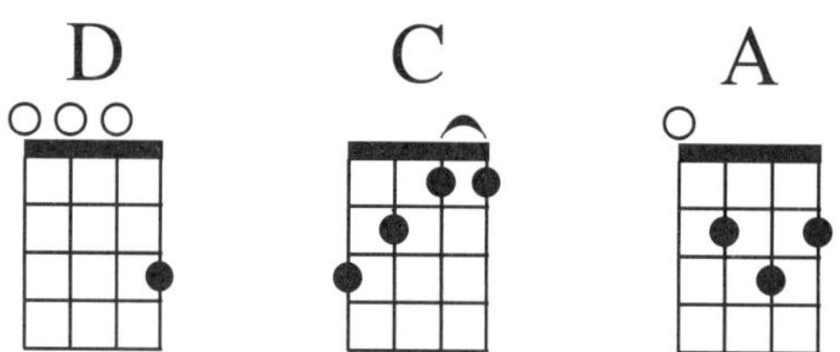

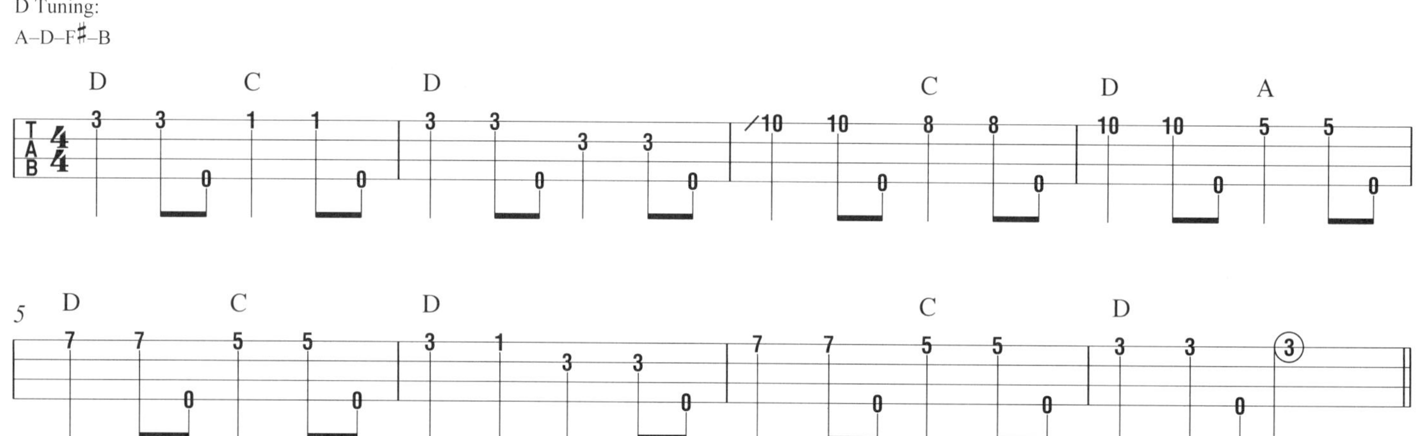

Lyrics:

Shoulder up your guns and call out your dog,
Shoulder up your guns and whistle up your dogs;
Goin' up the holler for to catch a ground hog,
Ground hog.

Yonder come Sally with a ten-foot pole,
Run here Sally with a ten-foot pole;
Get this ground hog out of his hole,
Ground hog.

Come here boys, come here quick,
Come here boys, come here quick;
This old ground hog thinks he's sick,
Ground hog.

Yonder come Molly with a smile and a grin,
Yonder come Molly with a smile and a grin;
Ground hog gravy all over her chin,
Ground hog.

WILDWOOD FLOWER

"Wildwood Flower" is a perennial classic of early American country music with its roots planted firmly in the sentimental song era of the late 1800s. Originally titled "I'll Twine Mid the Ringlets," it is a song of broken-hearted love that's usually played as an instrumental piece amongst guitar pickers and banjo enthusiasts alike. Be sure to listen to Maybelle Carter of the famous Carter Family pick this song on the guitar, as this is the quintessential source of inspiration for most fans of bluegrass and old-time music.

Remember to start by tuning your ukulele to D tuning: A–D–F♯–B. Count "1, 2" and then come in on the third beat, which is an open F♯ note. This piece has a nice feel to it with a varied combination of eighth notes, quarter notes, half notes, and whole notes.

D A7 G

Other great versions of this song that you might want to check out include renditions by Chet Atkins, Emmylou Harris, Flatt & Scruggs, Johnny Cash, Joan Baez, and Molly Tuttle.

KINISHINAI (NEVER MIND)

"Kinishinai" means "never mind" in Japanese. One day, I was noodling around on the ukulele, playing clawhammer, and a friend asked me what I was playing. When I couldn't think of a response, I just kept mumbling nonsense syllables, until finally, he said, "oh, never mind!" That's when I realized, "Never Mind" would make a great song title! Being a linguistics lover, I enjoy hearing what English words sound like when spoken in other languages. Since Japanese has always been a fascinating language to me, I named this cool piece in D tuning "Kinishinai."

This has a cool, plucked Japanese *koto* sound (stringed Japanese instrument) that's coupled with a simple pentatonic flavor and a bluesy part in 3rds. This is drone-less and is a fine example of a four-part tune played in an AABBCCD form. It has some different rhythms and slides that you'll need to pay attention to, but nothing too tricky. Remember to count "1 and, 2 and, 3 and, 4 and" in the fourth section.

D A7 D°7

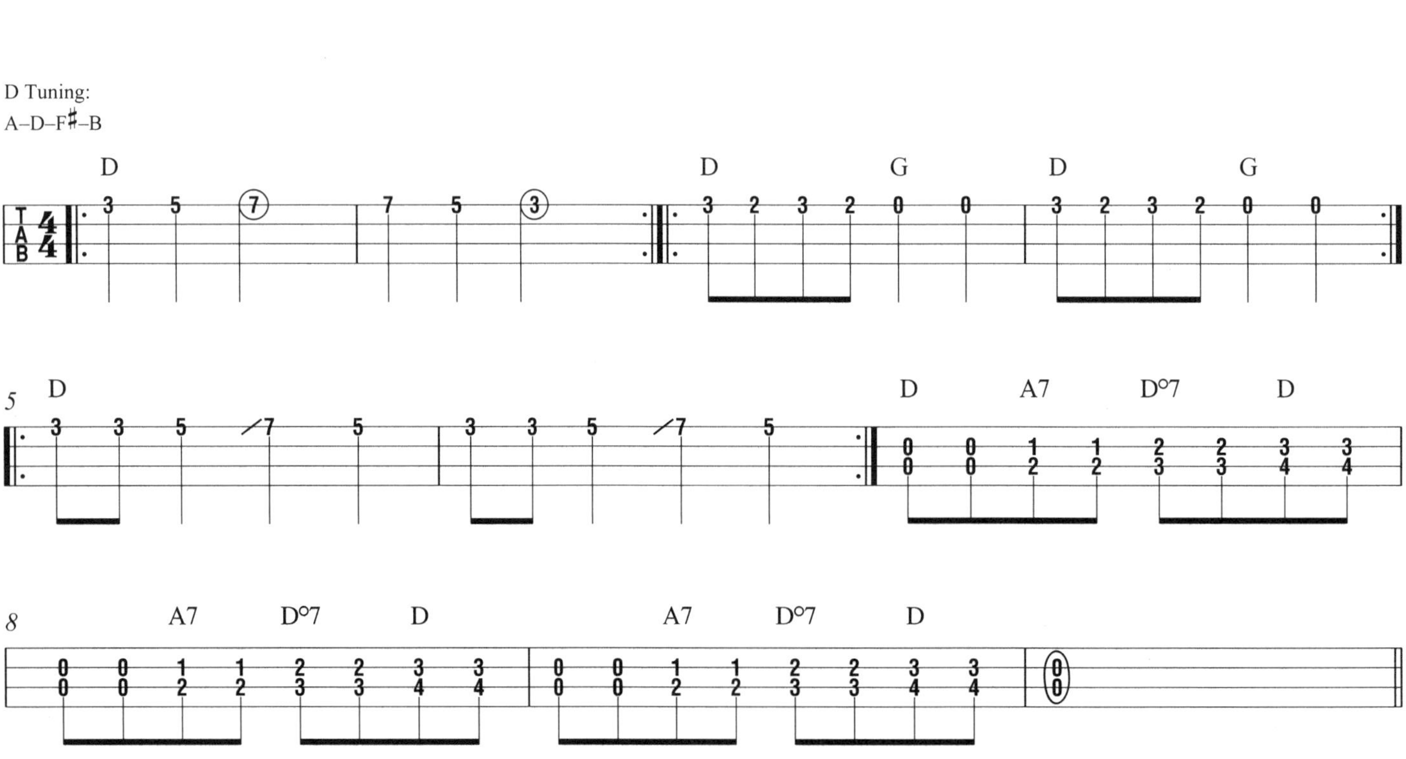

TERRY TIEHAN'S POLKA

Here's an excellent example of an Irish session tune that's super lively and incredibly well-suited for clawhammer. If you enjoy playing this kind of music, there are thousands of Irish polkas, waltzes, reels, airs, jigs, and hornpipes that are just waiting to be arranged for clawhammer.

This old dance melody is usually played in the key of A. In D tuning, familiar G shapes and positions from C tuning get raised one whole step to A, making this a dynamite piece to play using G shapes. In C tuning, the re-entrant G string provides the drone, so when it's raised one whole step, it becomes A and is therefore used to drone in D tuning.

This song has a two-part AABB form with a load of hammer-ons and pull-offs. Be sure to practice the accompaniment chords as well so you can move back and forth between melody and rhythm when playing in a session or jam.

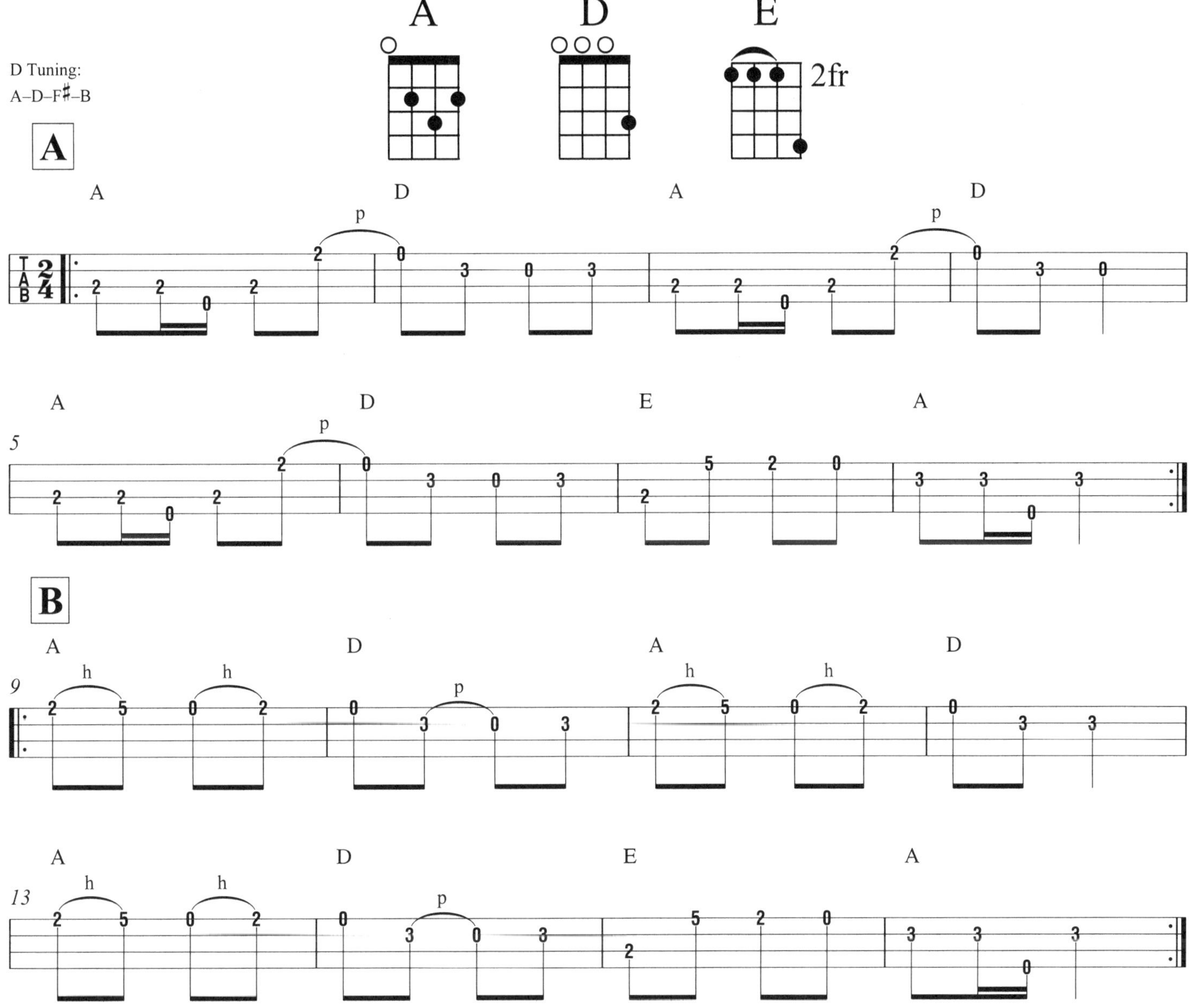

Irish Polkas

If you're looking for more tunes like "Terry Tiehan's Polka," then check out some of these traditional polkas that often appear at Irish jam sessions:

- "Britches Full of Stitches"
- "John Ryan's Polka"
- "The Church Street Polka"
- "The Kerry Polka"
- "Ballydesmond Polka No. 3"
- And many more, yet to be discovered!

HAMMOND BREAKDOWN

"Hammond Breakdown" is an up-tempo, fiddle-tune-inspired instrumental that includes slides, pull-offs, and basic drone techniques. It's played out of G shapes that sound in the key of A when re-tuned to D tuning. Be sure to watch the video a few times to soak up the rhythm and the feel of this tune.

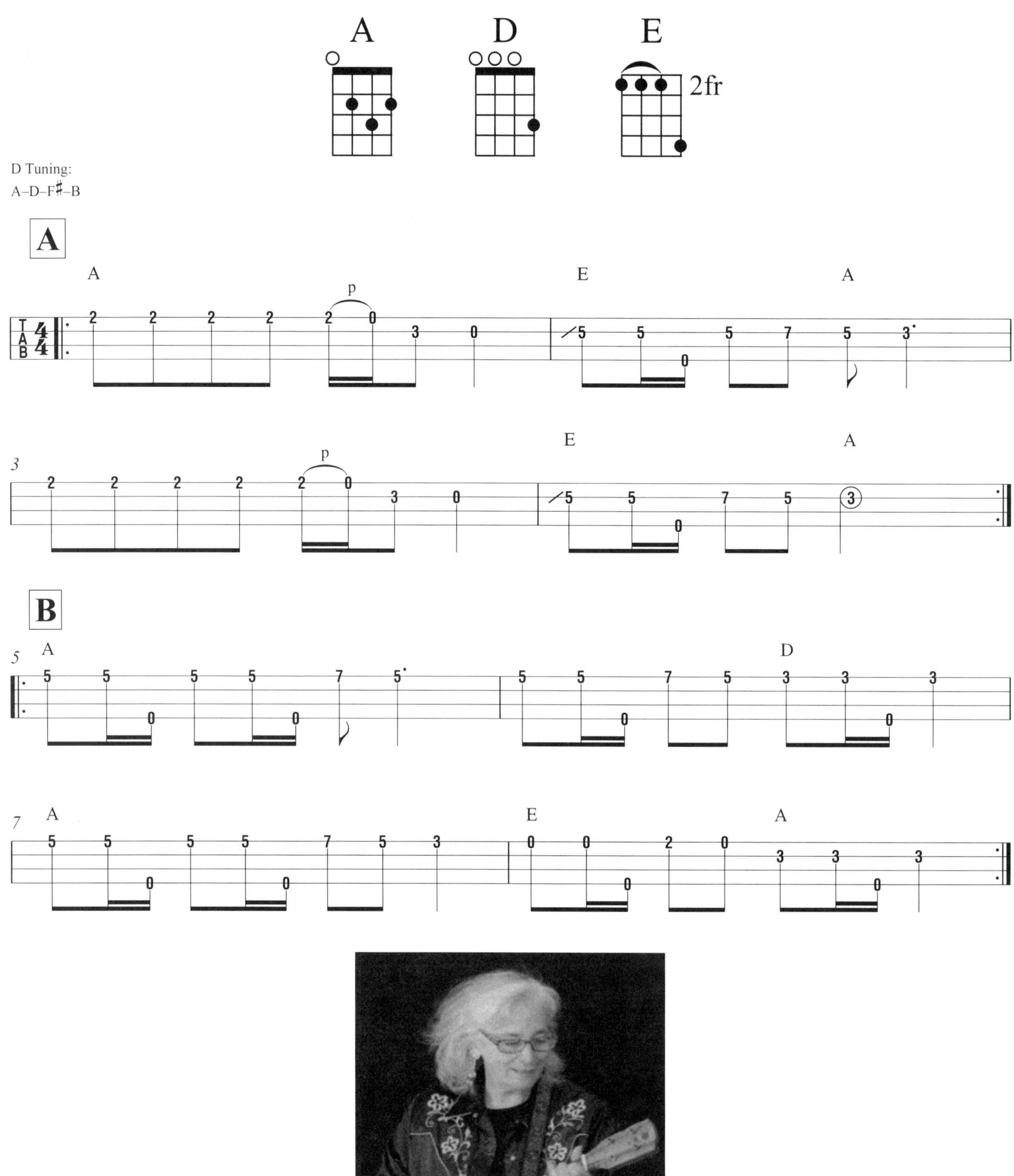

Be sure to check out clawhammer banjo and uke master Cathy Fink.
Photo by Irene Young.

PLAYING SONGS IN Gm TUNING (G–B♭–D–G)

As discussed earlier, clawhammer banjo music is a study in alternate tunings. The wealth of different tunings is truly astounding! Gm tuning is a great one to know for uke because it affords you the opportunity to use the high-G string for droning while also in a minor key. Here's how to re-tune to it from standard C tuning:

Gm Tuning: G–B♭–D–G

1. Start by tuning the C string (3rd string) down one whole step, from C to B♭.
2. Next, tune your E string (2nd string) down one whole step, from E to D.
3. Lastly, tune your A string (1st string) down one whole step from A to G.

ASHEVILLE JUNCTION

"Asheville Junction" (also known as "Swannanoa Tunnel") is said to date back to the late 1800s. Asheville Junction is located near Asheville, North Carolina, and is often associated with the banjo legend Bascom Lamar Lunsford. If you're a lover of old train songs like "Wabash Cannonball," "Wreck of the Old 97," or "Midnight Special," then "Asheville Junction" is a great find to add to your repertoire.

The melody for this tune stays on one string throughout, and other than a few added drones, it is fairly easy to play.

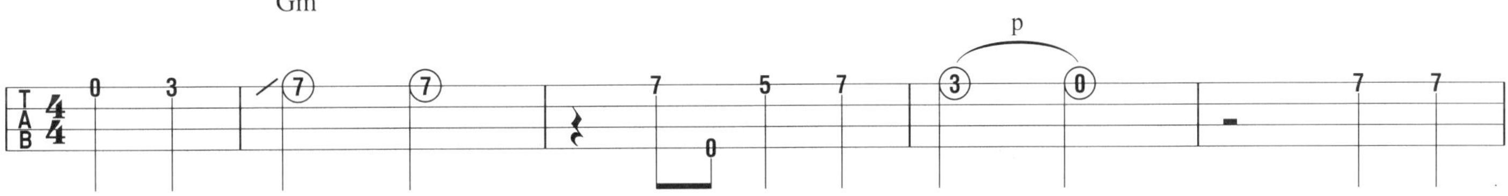

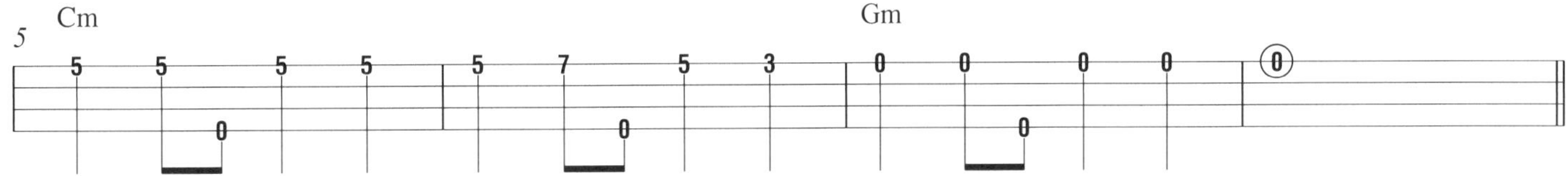

Lyrics:

Asheville Junction, Swannanoa Tunnel,
All caved in, baby, all caved in.

I'm going back to Swannanoa Tunnel,
That's my home, baby, that's my home.

When you hear that hoot owl squalling,
Somebody dying, baby, somebody dying.

Ain't no hammer in this mountain
Out-rings mine, baby, out-rings mine.

Last December, I remember
The wind blowed cold, baby, the wind blowed cold.

ZUM GALI GALI

"Zum Gali Gali" is a Hebrew folk staple from Israel, arranged here in Gm tuning. Often sung in a round, it sounds dynamite when played in a clawhammer style.

This is a drone-less, two-part melody that will allow you to focus on refining the "hammering" motion that underlies everything we do in the clawhammer style. Be sure to watch out for the dotted half notes in the B section. They have a value equal to three beats when played in a 4/4 measure.

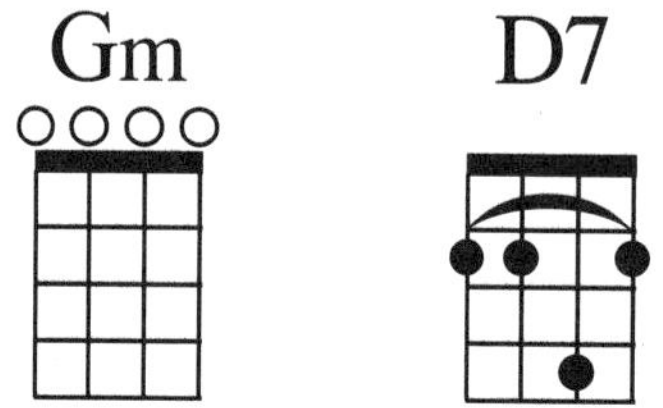

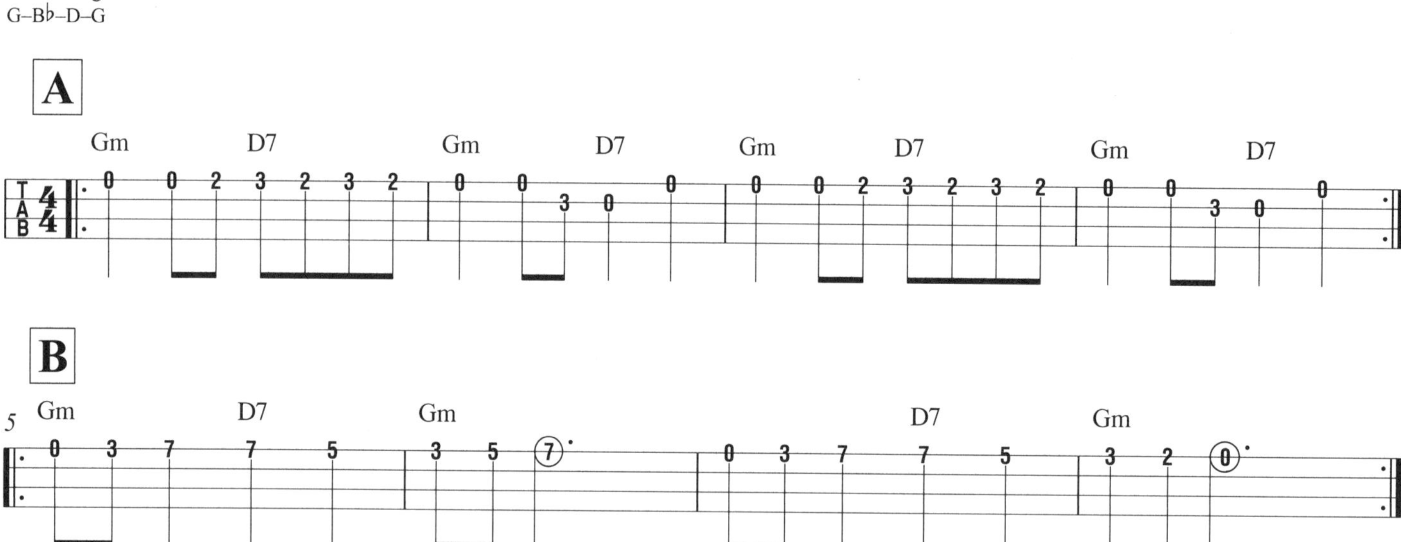

HINEI MA TOV

"Hinei Ma Tov" is a Hebrew folk tune with lyrics derived from Psalm 133:1. Often sung in a round, it is a beautiful melody that sounds fabulous in this rich-toned open tuning of Gm.

The time signature is 3/4, so remember to count "1, 2, 3" for each measure. Note that each section is repeated in an AABB song format. This is a drone-less melody that sounds great while giving you a nice workout of the "hammering" motion that we've been striving to perfect all along. Also, note the arrows that appear in the A section. These tell you to brush down across all four strings in one sweeping motion. Watch the video and review the earlier brush exercises to get a feel for how the brush stroke looks and sounds when done with good form.

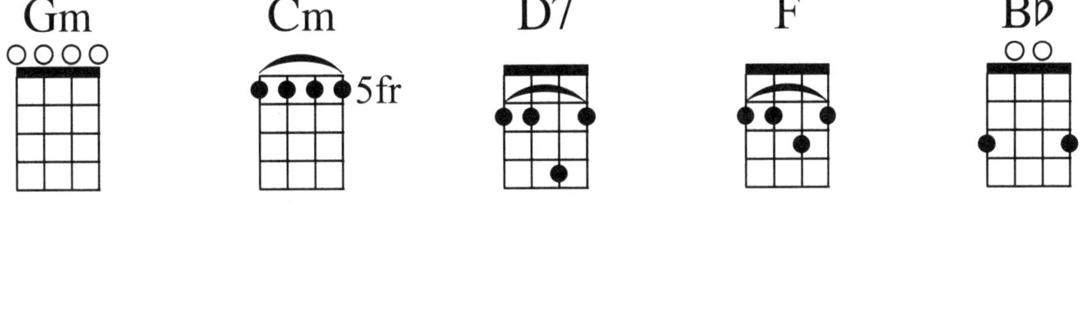

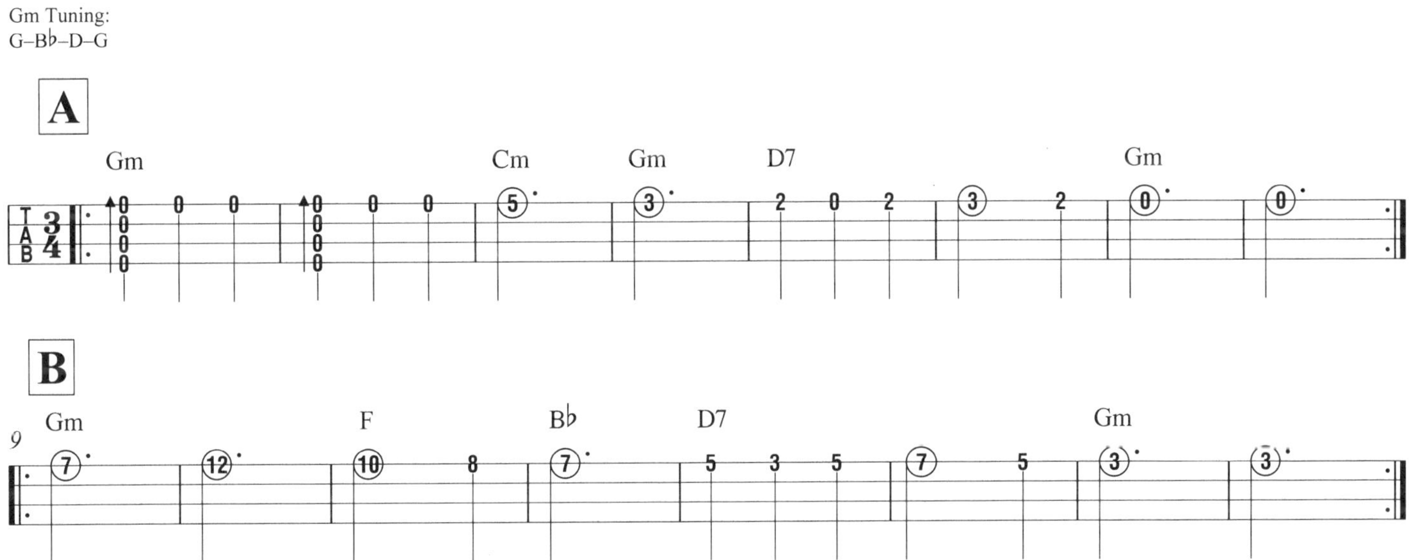

LEARNING SONG ACCOMPANIMENT PATTERNS

Next, we'll get back to standard C tuning and look at some different ways to use the clawhammer technique to accompany yourself or others (vocal or instrumental) with patterns that work well over many songs and styles.

PATTERN 1: 4/4 TIME

Pattern 1 is a basic alternating clawhammer stroke that moves back and forth between the C string and the E string. This pattern can be used in either C or D tuning to accompany your voice when singing.

You can certainly go back to basic down-up, down-up strumming to accompany your singing, but if you'd like to keep a clawhammer groove going, then you'll need to get comfortable combining the bum-ditty stroke with an alternating single-note/chord pattern. This is essentially the same pattern that you learned earlier in the book; the difference now is that you'll be alternating between different chord tones, followed by a joint brush stroke/drone combo.

To begin, practice song accompaniment Pattern 1 (below) a couple dozen times for each chord shown, counting "1, 2 and, 3, 4 and." Then, apply the pattern to "The Crawdad Song." We played this tune near the start of the book; now, try it out with this new backup pattern and see if you can sing and play it on your own!

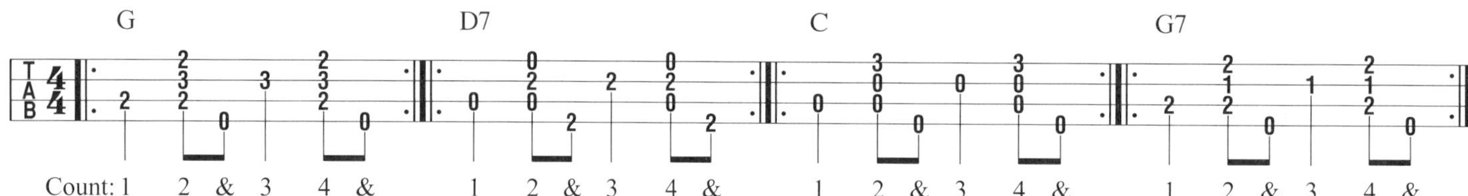

The Crawdad Song

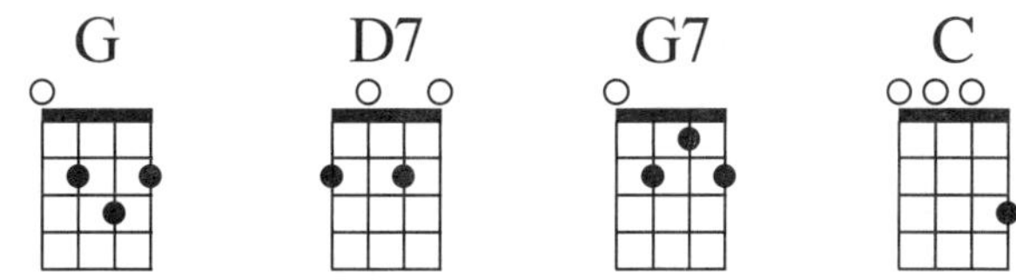

G
You get a line and I'll get a pole now, honey.

D7
Honey, you get a line and I'll get a pole now, babe, babe.

G G7 C
You get a line and I'll get a pole, we'll go fishing in the crawdad hole,

G D7 G
Honey, sugar baby, mine.

G
Yonder come a man with a sack on his back now, honey.

D7
Honey, yonder come a man with a sack on his back now, babe, babe.

G G7 C
Yonder come a man with a sack on his back, packing all the crawdads he can pack,

G D7 G
Honey, sugar baby, mine.

G
What you gonna do when the lake runs dry now, honey?

D7
Honey, what you gonna do when the lake runs dry now, babe, babe?

G G7 C
What you gonna do when the lake runs dry now, sit on the banks and watch the crawdads dry?

G D7 G
Honey, sugar baby, mine.

Going Down That Road Feeling Bad

Here's a bonus video of me playing backup with a clawhammer pattern while singing another old-time tune at a quicker tempo, with help from my friend Will Branch on guitar. You can see the clawhammer accompaniment pattern put to use when I'm singing, and then it switches back to the instrumental melody part between verses.

Using Pattern 1, let's try playing the old bluegrass favorite, "Hand Me Down My Walking Cane." This song goes back to the late 1800s and is a real classic in folk, old-time, and bluegrass circles. Check out versions by Norman Blake, Gid Tanner and the Skillet Lickers, Jerry Lee Lewis, and Ernest Stoneman, to name a few.

Hand Me Down My Walking Cane

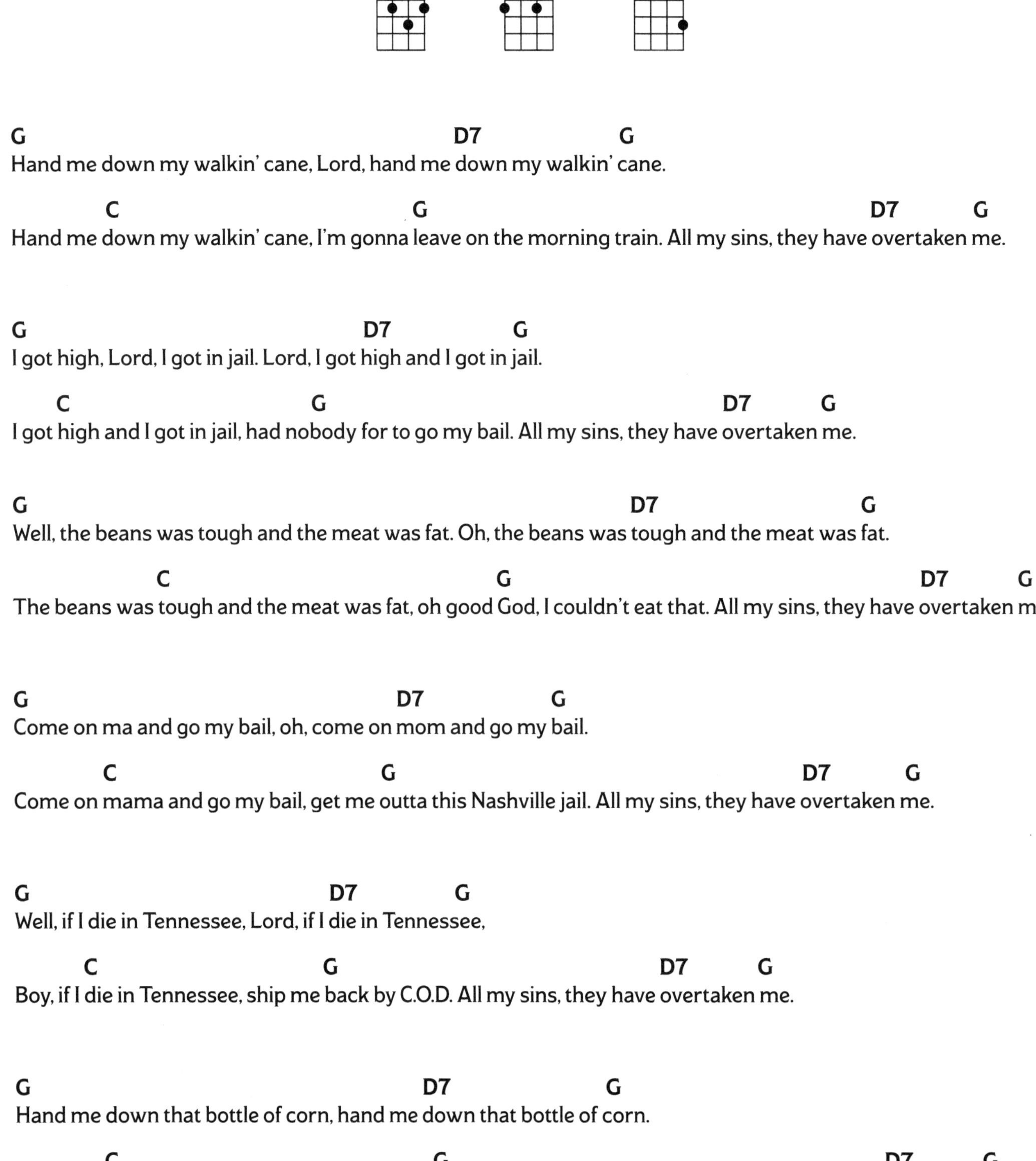


```
G                                              D7                 G
Hand me down my walkin' cane, Lord, hand me down my walkin' cane.

           C                                 G                                                   D7         G
Hand me down my walkin' cane, I'm gonna leave on the morning train. All my sins, they have overtaken me.
```

```
G                                      D7             G
I got high, Lord, I got in jail. Lord, I got high and I got in jail.

     C                        G                                           D7         G
I got high and I got in jail, had nobody for to go my bail. All my sins, they have overtaken me.
```

```
G                                                              D7                     G
Well, the beans was tough and the meat was fat. Oh, the beans was tough and the meat was fat.

                C                              G                                            D7        G
The beans was tough and the meat was fat, oh good God, I couldn't eat that. All my sins, they have overtaken me.
```

```
G                                         D7            G
Come on ma and go my bail, oh, come on mom and go my bail.

          C                       G                                        D7         G
Come on mama and go my bail, get me outta this Nashville jail. All my sins, they have overtaken me.
```

```
G                                D7          G
Well, if I die in Tennessee, Lord, if I die in Tennessee,

        C                        G                                D7        G
Boy, if I die in Tennessee, ship me back by C.O.D. All my sins, they have overtaken me.
```

```
G                                        D7                 G
Hand me down that bottle of corn, hand me down that bottle of corn.

          C                                   G                                               D7         G
Hand me down that bottle of corn, we'll have fun as sure as you're born. All my sins, they have overtaken me.
```

Check out my favorite version of this tune by flatpicking guitar master Norman Blake on YouTube. Search for "Norman Blake Hand Me Down My Walking Cane."

PATTERN 2: 3/4 WALTZ TIME

It doesn't matter what style of music that you choose to play on your ukulele, you'll always want to mix things up with a variety of time signatures and add a waltz or two to your repertoire. Waltz time is three beats per measure, typically counted "1, 2, 3," etc.

When you're playing a waltz in the clawhammer style, you'll count "1, 2 and, 3 and" for each measure. To start, keep your hand in a claw shape. Use your index finger to strike the chord tone then brush down-up, down-up for the subsequent eighth notes.

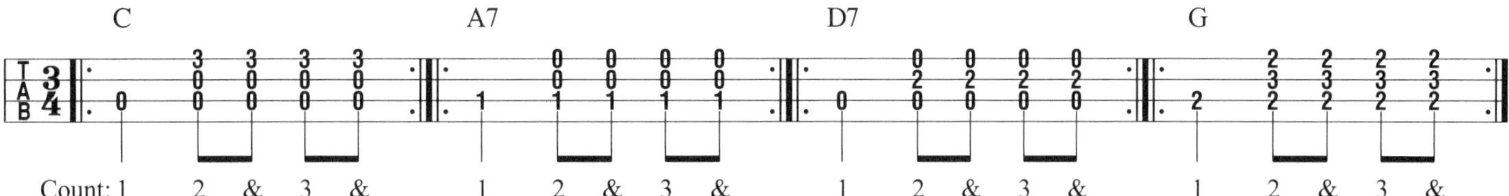

Now apply Pattern 2 as backup for the next several 3/4 songs. Try singing along!

My Bonnie Lies Over the Ocean

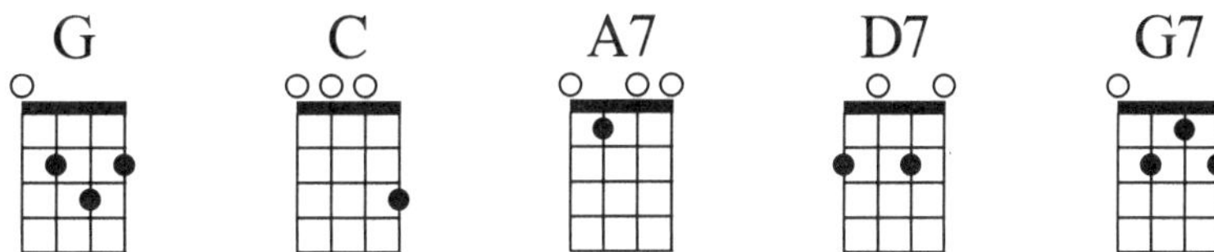

G C G A7 D7
My bonnie lies over the ocean, my bonnie lies over the sea.

G C G C D7 G
My bonnie lies over the ocean, bring back my bonnie to me.

G G7 C D7 G
Bring back, bring back, bring back my bonnie to me, to me.

G G7 C D7 G
Bring back, bring back, bring back my bonnie to me.

All the Good Times Are Past and Gone

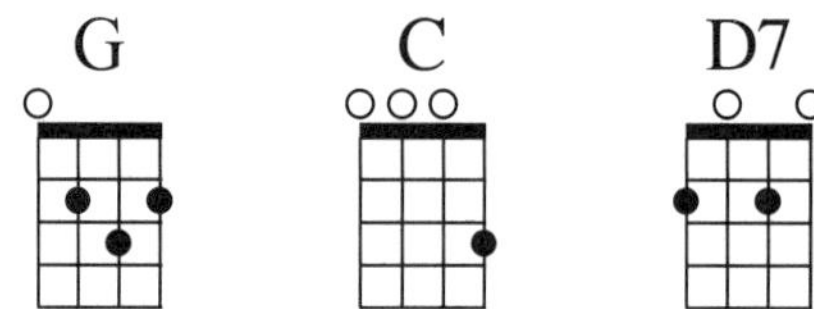

G **C** **G** **D7**
All good times are past and gone, all good times are over.

G **C** **G** **D7** **G**
All good times are past and gone, little darling don't you weep no more!

For those who are looking for more of a challenge, here's how you can add a drone to your waltz strum:

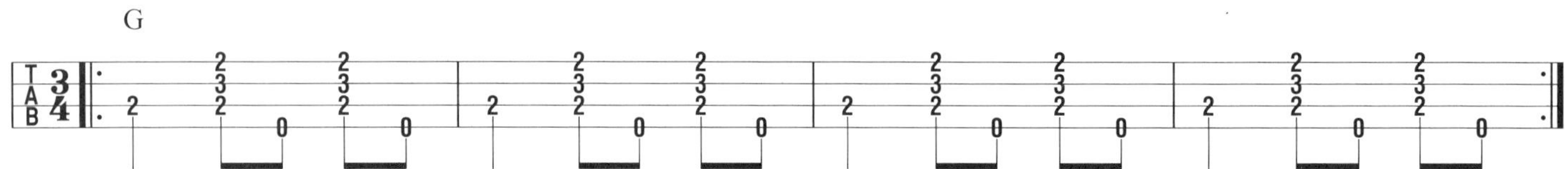

Now let's try it with the American folk song "Down in the Valley."

Down in the Valley

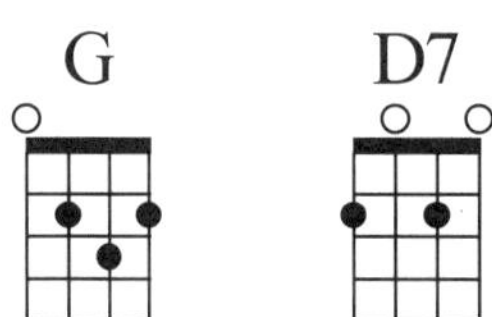

G **D7** **G**
Down in the valley, the valley so low, hang your head over, hear the wind blow.

D7 **G**
Hear the wind blow, dear, hear the wind blow, hang your head over, and hear the wind blow.

DRONING THE BOOGIE

Let's apply the clawhammer approach to "walking the boogie-woogie." Boogie-woogie grew out of the blues and ragtime piano traditions. As time went on, guitarists from every genre began to incorporate boogie-woogie into their styles. Today, the boogie sound is so iconic that almost everyone has heard a song that's rooted in boogie, from Jerry Lee Lewis playing "Whole Lot of Shakin' Going On" to Elvis Presley shaking his hips to "That's All Right." Today, elements of boogie have crept into almost every corner of American music.

The arrangement below is designed to give you a lot of practice refining your drone stroke. Note that every melody note is followed by a drone stroke. Practice this slowly at first; watch the video, listen closely, and count "1 and, 2 and, 3 and, 4 and." Note the shuffled, eighth-note rhythm feel of this song, which is heard in many blues, folk, jazz, and boogie tunes throughout recorded music history.

Droning the Boogie-Woogie Blues

Though you may not think of the banjo as a blues instrument, there are many great blues players who've incorporated the banjo into their performances, including the late John Jackson, Elizabeth Cotten, Gus Cannon, and Papa Charlie Jackson, to name a few! The syncopation that is inherent in the blues idiom makes it a given that we'd want to try and play boogie using the clawhammer tradition.

FAREWELL

If you've made it this far, then you've surely begun to realize that playing clawhammer on the ukulele is to immerse yourself in the world of the banjo and its influence on pop (and unpopular!) music culture. Congratulations! It's a rich tradition that you have now become a part of!

FURTHER READING

There has been much written about the evolution of the banjo and clawhammer, in particular. Below is a list that you can use as a springboard into the historical origins of the banjo in America. The story is fascinating at every turn!

- *America's Instrument: The Banjo in the Nineteenth Century* by Phillip F. Gura and James F. Bollman
- *African Banjo Echoes in Appalachia: A Study of Folk Traditions* by Cecelia Conway
- *Banjo Roots and Branches* by Robert B. Winans
- *Banjos: The Tsumura Collection* by Akira Tsumura
- *Banjo Aerobics: A 50-Week Workout Program for Developing, Improving and Maintaining Banjo Technique* by Michael Bremer
- *Blues Banjo: Lessons, Licks, Riffs, Songs and More* by Fred Sokolow
- *Building New Banjos for an Old-Time World* by Richard Jones-Bamman
- *Clawhammer Style Banjo: A Complete Guide for Beginning and Advanced Banjo Players* by Ken Perlman
- *Clawhammer Cookbook: Tools, Techniques & Recipes for Playing Clawhammer Banjo* by Michael Bremer
- *Hal Leonard Folk Banjo Method* by Michael Bremer
- *Ring the Banjar: The Banjo in America from Folklore to Factory* by Robert Lloyd Webb
- *The How and the Tao of Old Time Banjo* by Patrick Costello

I hope that this book has helped you to gain a solid understanding of the rudiments of clawhammer and your effort to play this style on the ukulele.

Claw-fully,

Lil' Rev

www.lilrev.com

Learn to play the **Ukulele** with these great Hal Leonard books!

Hal Leonard Ukulele Method

Book 1
by Lil' Rev
The Hal Leonard Ukulele Method is designed for anyone just learning to play ukulele. This comprehensive and easy-to-use beginner's guide by acclaimed performer and uke master Lil' Rev includes many fun songs of different styles to learn and play. The accompanying audio contains 46 tracks of songs for demonstration and play along. Includes: types of ukuleles, tuning, music reading, melody playing, chords, strumming, scales, tremolo, music notation and tablature, a variety of music styles, ukulele history and much more.
00695847 Book Only
00695832 Book/Online Audio
00320534 DVD

Book 2
00695948 Book Only
00695949 Book/Online Audio

Ukulele Chord Finder
00695803 9" x 12"
00695902 6" x 9"
00696472 Book 1 with Online Audio + Chord Finder

Ukulele Scale Finder
00696378 9" x 12"

Easy Songs for Ukulele
00695904 Book/Online Audio
00695905 Book

Ukulele for Kids
00696468 Book/Online Audio
00244855 Method & Songbook

Baritone Ukulele Method
00696564 Book/Online Audio

Bass Ukulele Method
00350667 Book/Online Audio

Jake Shimabukuro Teaches Ukulele Lessons
Learn notes, chords, songs, and playing techniques from the master of modern ukulele! In this unique book with online video, Jake Shimabukuro will get you started on playing the ukulele. The book includes full transcriptions of every example, the video features Jake teaching you everything you need to know plus video of Jake playing all the examples.
00320992 Book/Online Video

Fretboard Roadmaps – Ukulele
The Essential Patterns That All the Pros Know and Use
by Fred Sokolow & Jim Beloff
Take your uke playing to the next level! Tunes and exercises in standard notation and tab illustrate each technique. Absolute beginners can follow the diagrams and instruction step-by-step, while intermediate and advanced players can use the chapters non-sequentially to increase their understanding of the ukulele. The audio includes 59 demo and play-along tracks.
00695901 Book/Online Audio

Play Ukulele Today!
A Complete Guide to the Basics
by Barrett Tagliarino
This is the ultimate self-teaching method for ukulele! Includes audio with full demo tracks and over 60 great songs. You'll learn: care for the instrument; how to produce sound; reading music notation and rhythms; and more.
00699638 Book/Online Audio
00293927 Book 1 & 2/Online Media

Ukulele Aerobics
For All Levels, from Beginner to Advanced
by Chad Johnson
This package provides practice material for every day of the week and includes an online audio access code for all the workouts in the book. Techniques covered include: strumming, fingerstyle, slides, bending, damping, vibrato, tremolo and more.
00102162 Book/Online Audio

Do-It-Yourself Ukulele
The Best Step-by-Step Guide to Start Playing
by Terry Carter
Learn ukulele on your own terms with this incredibly helpful book. *Do-It-Yourself Ukulele* uses well-known pop, rock, blues, traditional, and Hawaiian tunes in its step-by-step instructions on what you need to know to get started and sounding like a pro in no time.
00359771 Book/Online Media

www.halleonard.com

Prices, contents and availability subject to change without notice.
Prices listed in U.S. funds.

1123
424

The Best Collections for Ukulele

The Best Songs Ever

70 songs have now been arranged for ukulele. Includes: Always • Bohemian Rhapsody • Memory • My Favorite Things • Over the Rainbow • Piano Man • What a Wonderful World • Yesterday • You Raise Me Up • and more.

00282413

Campfire Songs for Ukulele

30 favorites to sing as you roast marshmallows and strum your uke around the campfire. Includes: God Bless the U.S.A. • Hallelujah • The House of the Rising Sun • I Walk the Line • Wagon Wheel • You Are My Sunshine • and more.

00129170

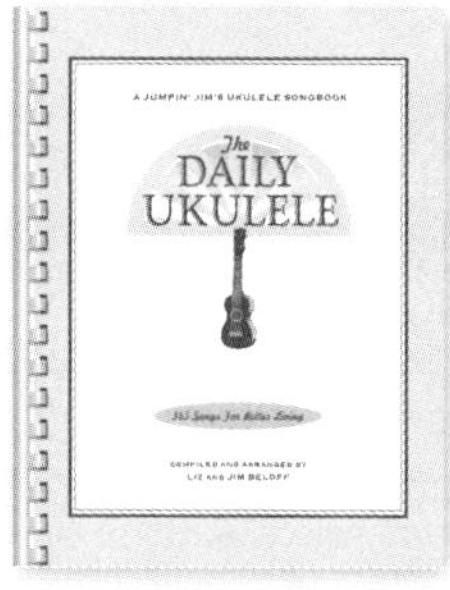

The Daily Ukulele

arr. Liz and Jim Beloff

Strum a different song everyday with easy arrangements of 365 of your favorite songs in one big songbook! Includes favorites by the Beatles, Beach Boys, and Bob Dylan, folk songs, pop songs, kids' songs, Christmas carols, and Broadway and Hollywood tunes, all with a spiral binding for ease of use.

00240356 Original Edition
00240681 Leap Year Edition
00119270 Portable Edition

Disney Hits for Ukulele

Play 23 of your favorite Disney songs on your ukulele. Includes: The Bare Necessities • Cruella De Vil • Do You Want to Build a Snowman? • Kiss the Girl • Lava • Let It Go • Once upon a Dream • A Whole New World • and more.

00151250

Also available:
00291547 Disney Fun Songs for Ukulele
00701708 Disney Songs for Ukulele
00334696 First 50 Disney Songs on Ukulele

First 50 Songs You Should Play on Ukulele

An amazing collec-tion of 50 accessible, must-know favorites: Hey, Soul Sister • I Walk the Line • I'm Yours • Imagine • Over the Rainbow • The Rainbow Connection • Riptide • and more.

00149250

Also available:
00292982 First 50 Melodies on Ukulele
00289029 First 50 Songs on Solo Ukulele
00347437 First 50 Songs to Strum on Uke

40 Most Streamed Songs for Ukulele

40 top hits that sound great on uke! Includes: Despacito • Feel It Still • Girls like You • Happier • Havana • High Hopes • The Middle • Perfect • 7 Rings • Shallow • Shape of You • Something Just like This • Stay • Sucker • Sunflower • Sweet but Psycho • Thank U, Next • Without Me • and more!

00298113

The 4 Chord Songbook

With just 4 chords, you can play 50 hot songs on your ukulele! Songs include: Brown Eyed Girl • Hey Ya! • Ho Hey • Jessie's Girl • Let It Be • One Love • Stand by Me • Toes • With or Without You • and many more.

00142050

Also available:
00141143 The 3-Chord Songbook

Pop Songs for Kids

30 easy pop favorites for kids to play on uke, including: Brave • Fight Song • Happy • Havana • House of Gold • How Far I'll Go • Let It Go • Rewrite the Stars • Roar • Shake It Off • What Makes You Beautiful • and more.

00284415

Simple Songs for Ukulele

50 favorites for standard G-C-E-A ukulele tuning, including: All Along the Watchtower • Can't Help Falling in Love • Don't Worry, Be Happy • Ho Hey • I'm Yours • King of the Road • Sweet Home Alabama • You Are My Sunshine • and more.

00156815

Also available:
00276644 More Simple Songs for Ukulele

Top Hits of 2022

This collection features 16 of today's top hits arranged with vocal melody, lyrics, and chord diagrams for standard G-C-E-A tuning for ukulele. Songs include: As It Was • Carolina • Enemy • Freedom • Glimpse of Us • Hold My Hand • Numb Little Bug • On My Way • and more.

01100312

Also available:
00355553 Top Hits of 2020
00302274 Top Hits of 2019

Ukulele: The Most Requested Songs

Strum & Sing Series
Cherry Lane Music

Nearly 50 favorites all expertly arranged for ukulele! Includes: Bubbly • Build Me Up, Buttercup • Georgia on My Mind • Your Body Is a Wonderland • and more.

02501453

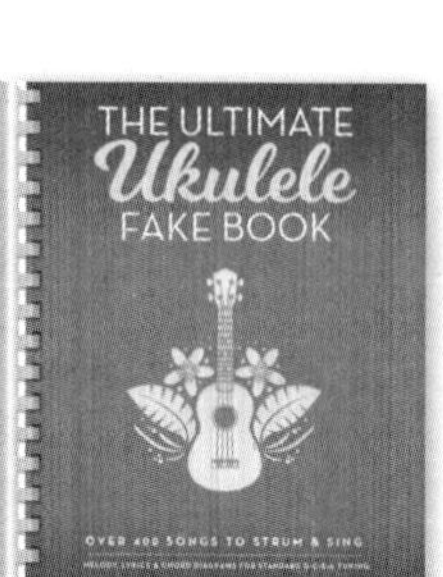

The Ultimate Ukulele Fake Book

Uke enthusiasts will love this giant, spiral-bound collection of over 400 songs for uke! Includes: Crazy • Dancing Queen • Downtown • Fields of Gold • Happy • Hey Jude • 7 Years • Summertime • Thinking Out Loud • Thriller • Wagon Wheel • and more.

00175500 9" x 12" Edition
00319997 5.5" x 8.5" Edition

Order today from your favorite music retailer at
halleonard.com

Prices, contents and availability subject to change without notice